Master the **3** core skills of selling:

## ASSESSMENT • PRESENTATION
## NEGOTIATION

# BRIDGING THE SELLING GAP

## Gerald G. Clerx

ISBN: 1470125463
ISBN-13: 9781470125462

# PREFACE

Our global economy is in transition and so too is the sales profession. *Competition* has given way to *collaboration*; *closing* has given way to *opening*; *selling* has given way to *serving*.

To successfully navigate this new consumer landscape your **attitude** must be rooted in a partnership mentality, your **aptitude** must include knowledge of your client's current reality situation and desired reality outcome and your **actions** must align with your client's goals and decision-making criteria.

This book will introduce you to the Gap Analysis Sales Model ©. This model is not just a strategy for selling success; it is a strategy for relationship and leadership success as well.

At its essence it's about providing others with a safe passage through challenging circumstances. The better we all understand it … the more we all embrace it and consistently deliver it … the greater the effect we make in this world and the more we all get in return.

As a colleague of mine Zig Ziglar once said, *"To get whatever you want in life, simply help enough other people get what they want in life."*

The content of this book will help you get more of what **you** want in **your** life by giving you the insights, skills and resources to help your clients get more of what **they** want in **their** lives.

# IS THIS BOOK FOR ME?

If you are in a client/ customer facing role, then *YES*! ... Unequivocally, unashamedly, unreservedly *YES*!

Excuse my apparent lack of humility but the reason why I say that with such certainty and conviction is because that is what thousands of course graduates have said about the content within this book and how it has accelerated their careers. When you have something that you know will enhance the lives of others, it's appropriate to be BOLD.

This book has been created for one purpose; *to accelerate YOUR selling success*, regardless of how many years you've been in the business. If you are new to the sales profession then this book represents a fresh clearing from which to launch a successful sales career. Those new to the business often get the best traction from core competency skill training because they have no "old school" habits to unlearn.

If you are a more experienced sales professional, you too will benefit tremendously from the contents found within. For you, this book represents a transition point in your career because regardless of how successful you have been to date, you will experience far greater success from this point forward.

Yes, it's true that you might have to unlearn some OLD school techniques that are no longer relevant in this NEW market economy but they will be replaced by a fresh set of practical skills and insights that are immediately applicable. The most common comment I receive from my more senior course graduates of this training series is, "This is the finest training I have received in my 20+ years in the business."

In fact, I believe so strongly in the content of this book that I will back my words with an unconditional guarantee. If you don't think the strategies in this book will immediately accelerate your selling success then return it for a full, no questions asked, refund.

So *"Yes"* ... **this book is definitely for you!** That's why it has found its way into your hand or onto your screen! Read it and take immediate control of your sales career.

Gerald G. Clerx

# DEDICATION

This book is dedicated to my inspiring wife and
business partner Shell, who is unrelenting
in her support toward my work and me.
Also to my THREE amazing children
Brayden, Sterling, and Alexia,
who remind me every day to
think BIG, be BOLD, and
DANCE like no one's watching.

# INTRODUCTION

## The GAP

The global economic downturn marked a critical crossroad for those within the sales profession. This event forever altered the consumer landscape and the sales model required to successfully navigate it.

Today, consumers are more skeptical, price conscious, product savvy and pressure resistant than at any other time in history. They don't want to be *cold called*, *up sold*, or *hard sold*. They don't want to be *trial closed*, *tie down closed*, or *Columbo closed*. They don't want *loss leaders*, *red herrings*, or *high pressure*. And they certainly don't want to be *nibbled*. These "old school" tactics have no place in this new consumer landscape.

A fresh new "partnership" approach to selling has officially trumped the old "salesmanship" approach of years past, and those organizations that make this transition will thrive and survive in this new global economy. Those who fail to adapt will continue to lose clients and soon find themselves out of business!

## The BRIDGE

A bridge serves a truly noble purpose: it takes people from *where they are* to *where they want to get to*, directly, reliably and consistently. Each one spans a gap, often over perilous terrain, offering its users a quicker and safer alternative to get to their desired destination.

This book serves a similar purpose: to take you from where you are in your sales career, to where you want to be, without having to endure the lost time and forfeited revenues resulting from failed client experiences. As Groucho Marx once said; "We should learn from the mistakes of others. We don't have time to make them all ourselves."

## – This book is YOUR success bridge! –

Although I am the architect of this bridge, I give much of the credit to the thousands of sales professionals and service providers whom I've met and trained over the years. Throughout the learning process, each one of them has helped to shape the Gap Analysis Sales Model © into its current form.

The stories I tell are real; the results I promise are achievable and in fact have been achieved by sales professionals from around the globe. This training series has been delivered in twenty countries to over eighty thousand sales professionals, many who now generate commissioned earnings in excess of two million dollars annually.

The one common thread linking top producers in any market is that they do three things better than their competitors. These three skill sets represent the core competencies of selling: ASSESSMENT skills, PRESENTATION skills, and NEGOTIATION skills.

As a point of fact, your professional success is a direct reflection of your competence in *assessing* client needs, *presenting* product/ service solutions, and *negotiating* collaborative outcomes. After all, this represents the value you bring to your profession and the more competent you are, the more sales success you'll experience. It's as simple as that!

### BRIDGING THE SELLING GAP *is three books in one.*

In **Part I** you'll learn how to accelerate your success by mastering the first core skill of selling: ASSESSMENT. In this part of the book, you will discover exactly what questions to ask to fully uncover the gap between your client's *current reality* condition and *desired reality outcome.* You'll also learn how to identify your client's buyer profile so that you'll understand what he/ she needs to *hear*, *see*, and *know* to support a favorable buying decision.

In **Part II** you'll learn how to accelerate your success by mastering the second core skill of selling: PRESENTATION. In fact, everything you do that *opens doors* and *closes deals* comes down to your ability to communicate yourself and your product/ service offering to another person in a way that compels them to take a favorable course of action. In this part of the book you'll learn how to *tailor your content, structure your message* and *strengthen your delivery*.

In **Part III** you'll learn how to accelerate your success by mastering the third core skill of selling: NEGOTIATION. Understand that there are only three reasons why a transaction will falter once it enters this phase of the Gap Analysis Sales Model ©. In this part of the book, you will discover what these three potential deal breakers are, how to recognize them, and more importantly, how to respond to them when they are encountered.

The Gap Analysis Sales Model © is helping sales professionals "bridge their success gap" at a global level. The skills, insights and strategies from this training series have accelerated the success of sales professionals from around the world.

Now for the first time, the principles of the Gap Analysis Sales Model © is available to you in this landmark book. **Read it and seize immediate control of your sales career!**

# CONTENTS

## PART III ~ THE NEGOTIATION PHASE

# PART 1
# THE ASSESSMENT PHASE

In this part of the book you will learn how to *align*
your business, *profile* your clients and
comprehensively *assess* their
product/ service gap.

# INTRODUCTION TO ASSESSMENT

The first phase of the Gap Analysis Sales Model © is the ASSESSMENT Phase.

> ➤ Have you ever had a client fail to take action on a product/ service she should have acquired?
> ➤ Have you ever spent a lot of time with a client who you later discovered had neither the finances nor motivation to take action?
> ➤ Have you ever had a client tell you exactly what he/she wanted and yet went out and bought something completely different ... from one of your competitors?

... If you answered "yes" to any of these questions then you've suffered the consequences of a failed assessment. Know with absolute certainty that the success of your product/service presentation is built upon the foundation of your assessment.

---

### ASSESSMENT TIP:

**The success of your product/ service presentation is built upon the foundation of your assessment.**

---

A well-conducted assessment provides you with a solid footing from which to design and deliver a custom tailored and product-specific sales presentation. Reflect on that fact, because it's critical to your success that you understand it. You can't prescribe an effective solution if you haven't accurately diagnosed the problem.

The purpose of this part of the book is to accelerate your success by providing you with the *insights, skills, and resources to align your business, profile your clients and comprehensively assess their product/ service gap.*

In Chapter One you'll be introduced to an assessment tool that will help to establish your preferred style of selling (sales profile). Armed with this information you'll be better able to define your personal brand and align your sales activities accordingly to ensure a successful, lasting, and enjoyable career.

You will discover that your unique sales profile has specific *strengths* and *limitations* which, when understood, enables you to build your business around them accordingly.

In Chapter Two you'll learn how to uncover your client's preferred style of buying by observing *verbal, vocal,* and *visual* communication patterns.

You have no doubt discovered that each one of your clients is uniquely different. You can say one thing to one client and he will feel utterly compelled to take action, yet that identical message delivered to another will leave her completely uninspired. Why is that? It all comes down to psychometric differences. These differences influence what the client needs to *hear, see* and *know* to justify a purchase decision.

You'll discover why, once a client's **DISC** profile is known, her buying preferences becomes predictable, with an accuracy level approaching 90 percent.

Equipped with this insight, you'll be better positioned to design and deliver a winning sales presentation.

In Chapter Three you'll discover a questioning strategy designed to accurately define your client's *current* and *desired reality.*

Sales professionals must have absolute certainty regarding both these reference points. Why? Because the difference between them represents the gap! This gap constitutes the problem, which can only be successfully bridged if both coordinates are known.

Depending on the complexity of your product/ service offering it might be necessary to obtain over fifty separate pieces of information to fully assess your client's gap. Anything less would constitute an inconclusive assessment and compromise your ability to present a compelling solution.

In summary, the biggest mistakes sales professionals make during the ASSESSMENT phase of selling are:

- They fail to recognize their own strengths and limitations and neglect to align their businesses accordingly.
- They fail to establish their client's unique sales profile.
- They fail to accurately assess their client's product/ service gap.

The Acceleration Strategies that follow will bridge these competency gaps by providing you with the tools to master the core skill of ASSESSMENT.

THE ASSESSMENT PHASE

~Chapter One~

# Understanding Your Selling Style

*Accelerate your success by aligning your business activities with your selling style.*

૭૦

*"What you are speaks so loudly, I can't hear what you are saying."*
—Ralph Waldo Emerson

> *"Psychometrics helps us to understand why
> we do what we do ... and why others don't."*
> – Gerald G. Clerx

# WHAT IS MY SALES PROFILE?

## The GAP

Most sales professionals fail to understand that *who they are* influences *how they sell* and that *how they sell* influences *who will buy from them, who won't, and why.* This lack of awareness results in sales professionals failing to structure their business around their naturally occurring strengths.

## The BRIDGE

Psychometrics is the study of human behavior. It reveals why you do what you do and why others do it differently. It provides you with insights into your behavioral assets and identifies the value you bring to your team and your profession. While there are a number of psychometric assessment tools on the market, the easiest to apply, in my opinion, is the **DISC** system of human behavior. **DISC**, as a theory, was legitimized by the work of Dr. William Moulton Marston. Marston was an American psychologist who introduced the predictability of human behavior in his book "The Emotions of Normal People." Although this book was written in 1928 its findings are just as relevant today as they were then, especially as it applies to the psychology of selling.

**DISC** is an acronym that stands for **D**ominance, **I**nfluence, **S**teadiness, and **C**ompliance. Each characteristic represents one component of your behavioral makeup that collectively defines your psychometric profile. Once you know your own **DISC** profile you're in a position to structure your work environment accordingly.

DISC unravels the mysteries of human behavior. It's not just a relationship tool; it's also a marketing tool. Virtually every product manufacturer uses psychometrics as a resource to help them design products and target promotional efforts. Companies use it to hire candidates who are the best behavioral match for the job. Counselors use it to provide relationship advice, team builders use it to build effective teams, and I use it to show sales professionals how to accelerate their selling success.

---

**ASSESSMENT TIP:**

**Once you know your DISC profile
you can create a sales environment
that supports your naturally
occurring strengths.**

---

First, let's begin by obtaining some insights into your sales profile. Why is that important? Because who you are influences how you engage with others. You'll know this to be true. Think about it: when selling, you naturally hit it off with some clients—you establish instant rapport—you speak in a way that is easy for them to hear and in a way that they need to hear it. In fact, everything you do, think, and say is in alignment with him or her, and the client engagement process unfolds effortlessly.

Unfortunately the opposite is also true. You can likely recall times interacting with a client with whom you were completely out of sync. In this instance, nothing seemed to flow and the sales experience was downright arduous. If you've ever had a client respond to your proposal with "I'll think it over and get back to you," or "I'll call you when I am ready to make a decision," or "Thanks, leave it with me," it's the client's subtle way of letting you know that your presentation content and/ or delivery style did not align with his/ her unique decision-making needs.

So how do you determine your sales profile? A traditional psychometric questionnaire would take about ten minutes to complete. The responses would then be fed into a computer to tally the results and generate a comprehensive written report. However, in the interest of time and logistics I invite you to define your sales profile by reflecting on the following sets of descriptive adjectives and selecting the group that you feel best describes you, in your current sales role.

- The *first* group of descriptive adjectives is "demanding, ambitious, daring, restless, and assertive."
- The *second* group of descriptive adjectives is "influencing, optimistic, enthusiastic, persuading, and charming."
- The *third* group is "steady, deliberate, patient, accommodating, and sincere."
- The *fourth* group is "cautious, logical, precise, doubting, and perfectionist."

Select the one group of descriptors that you feel best describes you overall—not how you would like to be, nor how family members would describe you, but how you really see yourself in your current sales role.

If you feel the first group best describes you then write down or remember the capital letter "D" (Dominance). This is likely your primary behavioral characteristic. If you feel the second group best describes you overall then write down or remember the capital letter "I" (Influence). If it is the third group then write down the capital letter "S" (Steadiness) and if the forth group, the letter "C" (Compliance).

Now reflect again on the remaining three sets of descriptive adjectives. Select the group that is second most like you and place that secondary letter next to the primary letter. For instance you might be *primary* "**D**" and *secondary* "**I**," or *primary* "**S**" *secondary* "**C**." Once you know your *primary* and *secondary* behavioral characteristics you will begin to see why you connect with some people and why you don't with others.

It's important to note that your profile is a blend of all four characteristics, but it is the relationship between your *primary* and *secondary* that has the greatest impact on your sales profile.

In reality you have three separate profiles. In **DISC** these are referred to as your "work mask", your "self-image mask", and your "behavior under pressure mask." You transition between these "masks" depending on where you are and what you are doing. In this book, however, I will only make reference to your "work mask." If you'd like to obtain a more comprehensive report on your unique behavioral profile, check out the "Resources" section.

## Dominance

If you selected the "**D**" list of descriptors as being most like you then you likely have a high Dominance sales profile.

Dominance is a reflection of how a person responds to ***power***. High Dominance people are *actively* paced and *task* focused. Examples of public figures who are believed to have high Dominance profiles include Donald Trump, Hillary Clinton and Simon Cowell. High Dominance individuals are often found in leadership positions; because that is their preferred role.

## Influence

If you selected the "**I**" list of descriptors and as being most like you then you likely have a high Influence sales profile.

Influence is a reflection of how a person responds to ***people***. High Influence people are *actively* paced and *socially* focused. Examples of public figures who are believed to have high Influence profiles include people like Jay Leno, Ellen Degeneres and American Idol host Ryan Seacrest. High Influence individuals are typically found in the sales profession, in public relation positions, or in the role of talk show hosts.

## Steadiness

If you selected the "S" list of descriptors as being most like you then you likely have a high Steadiness profile.

Steadiness is a reflection of how a person responds to **pace.** High Steadiness people are *passively* paced (deliberate) and *socially* focused. Examples of public figures who are believed to have high Steadiness profiles include Nicole Kidman, Tom Hanks, Natalie Portman, and most professional golfers. High Steadiness profiles are more patient and nurturing than Dominance and Influence profiles; Steadiness people are typically found in occupations or roles that are in service to others. The health care industry and teaching professions are both strongly represented by members of this profile group.

## Compliance

If you selected the "C" list of descriptors as being most like you then you likely have a high Compliance profile.

Compliance is a reflection of how a person responds to **policy.** High Compliance people are *passively* paced (methodical) and *task* focused. Examples of public figures who are believed to have high Compliance profiles include Mark Zuckerberg, Al Gore and Bill Gates.

Since high Compliance individuals are strongly policy and procedure driven, we typically find them in highly structured professions or roles. The accounting and engineering professions are dominated by members of this profile group, as too are those in CFO positions.

In the following four Assessment Strategies, I will introduce you to the unique strengths and limitations of each sales profile so that you can structure your business accordingly.

---

## ASSESSMENT ACTION PLAN

---

**INSIGHTS:**

Know that your **DISC** profile impacts how you sell, how clients respond to you and the strengths you bring to your profession.

**SKILLS:**

Apply **DISC** awareness to help you structure your business to align with your natural occurring selling strengths.

**RESOURCES:**

Refer to the *Sales Profiling Tool* to help you understand your selling style. Go to www.theGAPanalysis.com and click on "Resources" page to learn more.

> *"If winning isn't everything, why do they keep score?"*
> – Vince Lombardi

# JUST DO IT!

### The GAP

Some high Dominance sales professionals fail to recognize the inherent strengths and limitations of their sales profile and subsequently neglect to align their business accordingly.

### The BRIDGE

Do you dislike losing, refuse to wait in line, loathe being told what to do, and resent having someone else be in control of your environment? If so, chances are very good you profile high in Dominance.

Those who profile high in Dominance are known as high D's. In the purest sense they are described as being *forceful, determined, inquisitive, restless, assertive, ambitious, demanding* and *competitive*. Evidence confirms that D's prefer a fast-paced environment that is ripe with challenges. Let's look at some of the behavioral assets and liabilities of sales professionals with high D profiles.

Behavioral assets that accelerate the high D's selling success include:

- ☺ Generating results in the face of opposition
- ☺ Figuring out ways to move the process forward
- ☺ Questioning the status quo and implementing new standards accordingly
- ☺ Taking on challenging situations with confidence and speed
- ☺ Taking control of and leading others

D profiles accelerate their success by their naturally occurring abilities during each of the three phases of the Gap Analysis Sales Model ©:

> During the ASSESSMENT phase, D's are highly skilled at getting right to the point. They don't waste time and aren't afraid to ask pointed and probing questions to accurately and efficiently uncover the client's product/ service gap.

> During the PRESENTATION phase, D's are known to communicate the merits of their product/ service offering in a bold and forthright manner. They speak with certainty and conviction, instilling confidence in others. They are also very efficient in their use of time and are not afraid to ask for the business at the conclusion of their presentation.

> During the NEGOTIATION phase, D's are skilled at overcoming opposition. They are outcome-oriented and constantly move the ball toward the goal line. If they encounter resistance during their end zone drive they're not afraid to push through the obstacle, however challenging. A common D response to a stalled negotiation is "Leave it with me and I'll figure something out" or "What's it going to take?"

High D's make excellent sales professionals, especially when engaged in activities that align with their naturally direct sales profile.

---

**ASSESSMENT TIP:**

**High D's make excellent sales professionals, especially when engaged in activities that align with their naturally direct sales profile.**

---

Just as **D**'s have naturally occurring behavioral assets, so too do they have liabilities that can decelerate their selling success. These include:

- ☹ Being impatient with the behavior of other non-**D** profiles
- ☹ Communicating in a blunt and often sarcastic manner
- ☹ Finding fault in others' actions or inactions
- ☹ Resisting participation in a team, unless in a leadership role
- ☹ Overriding the opinions and actions of others

There are four primary **D** profiles. They are:

## The Pure D

If your profile is strong on **D** and little else then you have a "Pure **D**" profile. This profile is accurately portrayed by the Ari Gold character from the HBO series *Entourage*. Members of this profile group are known for their rather unique sayings, some of which include: "If I want your opinion, I'll give it to you," and "The firings will continue until morale improves."

Here are the basic behavioral pairing of this profile group and the corresponding value these combinations bring to specific roles and teams.

## The DI

If your profile is primary **D** with secondary **I**, then you are affectionately referred to as the "Director." This behavioral pairing combines the qualities of *competitiveness* and *directness* with *friendliness* and *persuasion*. Richard Branson, Ronald Reagan, and Mark Cuban are thought to be members of this profile group. If this is your profile then your greatest asset is your ability to come up with unique and imaginative solutions to gaps in the market.

As a member of this profile group, you have been gifted with the ability to gain the willing cooperation of others, which makes you extremely effective at encouraging others to follow your lead.

In a team environment, you are known as the "go to person" when it comes to finding creative solutions to client problems.

## The DS

If your profile is primary **D** with secondary **S,** then you are a rare individual indeed. Very few people have this profile combination; however, those who do are sometimes referred to as "Human Pit Bulls." This pairing blends the high **S** qualities of *persistence* and *determination* with the high **D**'s *competitive resolve,* resulting in people who, once they sink their teeth into a goal or task, will refuse to give up until the goal has been realized or the task completed. Jack Nicklaus, Serena Williams, and Raphael Nadal are believed to share this combination profile.

In a team environment, you are the "go to person" when something needs to get done and nobody else has the intestinal fortitude to carry it through to completion.

## The DC

If your profile is primary **D** and secondary **C,** you're known as the "Lone Ranger." This behavioral pairing combines the qualities of *competitiveness* and *directness* with *precision* and *accuracy*. Dick Cheney and Hillary Clinton, in their public persona, appear to share this "calculating" combination. If this is your profile then you are known for your willingness to take direct action when there is little or no precedence set. In a team environment, you're the "go to person" when it comes time to making and enforcing unpopular decisions.

If you have a high **D** sales profile, recognize that you bring uniquely specific strengths to your profession and value to your team. Ensure that you direct your work efforts toward those activities that are supported by your naturally occurring behavioral assets.

---

### ASSESSMENT ACTION PLAN

---

○—▸INSIGHTS:

Know that D sales professionals accelerate their success when in a fast paced environment that is ripe with challenges.

○—▸SKILLS:

Apply the principles of DISC to help you structure your business activities to align with your Dominance level.

# THIS'LL BE FUN!

### The GAP

Some high Influence sales professionals fail to recognize the inherent strengths and limitations of their sales profile and subsequently neglect to align their business accordingly.

### The BRIDGE

Can you talk your way out of just about any situation? Do you sometimes even surprise yourself with your *gift of the gab*? Do you love to share your opinion with others and find yourself quick to fill a conversational void? Do you often forget the name of the person whom you were just introduced to and recover with a generic name like "Buddy" or "Pal"?

If you answered, "yes" to the bulk of these questions then chances are you profile high in Influence.

High I's are described as being *outgoing, talkative, friendly, charming, confident, positive, convincing,* and *communicative.* Evidence confirms that I's accelerate their success when engaged in activities that involve the participation of others in a social environment. Let's look at the assets and liabilities of sales professionals with high I profiles.

Behavioral assets that accelerate their selling success include:

- ☺ Inspiring others to take action
- ☺ Developing relationships easily
- ☺ Expressing their service offering with confidence
- ☺ Making favorable first impressions
- ☺ Communicating in an engaging and interactive manner

I's accelerate their success by their naturally occurring skills during each of the three phases of the Gap Analysis Sales Model ©:

> During the ASSESSMENT phase, I's are naturally skilled at breaking the ice and building rapport. They have the ability to talk to just about anyone on just about any topic in just about any place at any time. They are also gifted at asking the right questions to find commonality and develop the relationship.

> During the PRESENTATION phase, I's are effective at communicating with confidence. They are in their element when presenting their product/ service offering to the market. They're also known for communicating with an optimistic and enthusiastic vocal tone that's particularly pleasing to other members of this profile group.

> During the NEGOTIATION phase, I's negotiate with an attitude of positive expectancy. They are *open, optimistic,* and *enthusiastic.* You'll often hear encouraging phrases such as "Let's do this," "We'll figure something out," "Don't worry about it," "I'm on it," and the infamous "TRUST ME!" They have a knack for keeping things light even when the negotiation gets heavy.

High I's make brilliant sales professionals, especially when engaged in activities that align with their naturally outgoing sales profile.

---

**ASSESSMENT TIP:**

**High I's make brilliant sales professionals, especially when engaged in activities that align with their naturally outgoing sales profile.**

---

Just as I's have naturally occurring behavioral assets that accelerate their success, so too do they have liabilities that can decelerate their success. These include:

- ☹ Behaving impulsively at times
- ☹ Lacking direction and focus
- ☹ Failing to ask the important questions (for fear of rejection)
- ☹ Being inattentive to details
- ☹ Using time ineffectively

## The Pure I

There are four primary I profiles. The first is the "Pure I." These people are known for being outgoing, gregarious, charming, and often times a little "out there." Jim Carey, Robin Williams, and Russell Brand, in their public personas, are each believed to share the "Pure I" behavioral profile.

Here are the behavioral pairings of this profile group and the corresponding value these combinations bring to a specific role or team.

## The ID

If your profile is primary I with secondary D, then you are known as the "Promoter." This behavioral pairing combines *friendliness* and *persuasion* with *assertiveness* and *competitiveness*. It is the most common pairing within this profile group. John F. Kennedy, Oprah Winfrey, and Barack Obama are all believed to share this behavioral pairing. If this is your profile then your greatest behavioral asset is your ability to initiate contact with people and inspire them to take action.

In a team environment you are the "go to person" when it comes time to *opening doors* and *engaging others*.

## The IS

If your profile is primary I with secondary S, then you are known as the "Mediator." Ellen Degeneres, Jay Leno, and *Morning*

*Express* anchor Robin Meade are believed to be members of this profile group. If this is your profile, you are known for being naturally gifted at communicating ideas and developing lasting relationships. This behavioral pairing combines *friendliness* and *persuasion* with *deliberateness* and *dependability*.

In a team environment you are the "go to person" when it comes time to networking and managing on-going relationships.

## The IC

If your profile is primary **I** and secondary **C** you are known as the "Consultant." This behavioral pairing combines *friendliness* and *persuasion* with an attention to *detail* and *logic*. Many business strategists and medical equipment consultants share this behavioral pairing. If this is your profile then you have a natural ability to communicate complex ideas with accuracy and comprehension.

In a team environment you are the "go to person" when it comes time to motivating people to act on a technical or complex proposal.

If you have either of these high **I** sales profiles, recognize that you bring uniquely specific strengths to your profession and value to your team. Ensure that you direct your work efforts toward those activities that are supported by your naturally occurring behavioral strengths.

---

## ASSESSMENT ACTION PLAN

---

**○━INSIGHTS:**

Know that high **I** sales professionals accelerate their success when they are engaged in activities that involve the participation of others in a non-antagonistic environment.

**○━SKILLS:**

Apply the principles of **DISC** to help you structure your business activities to align with your Influence level.

> *"Slow down you move too fast,*
> *you've got to make the morning last."*
> — Paul Simon

# WHENEVER YOU'RE READY!

## The GAP

Some high Steadiness sales professionals fail to recognize the inherent strengths and limitations of their sales profile and subsequently neglect to align their business accordingly.

## The BRIDGE

Do you hate to be rushed into making a decision? Do you resist change and favor the status quo? Are you better one-on-one than in a group setting? Are you a better listener than you are a talker? When a friend gets cut, do you start to bleed? Are you extremely loyal to your family members, close friends, and the company you represent?

If these statements are true for you then you are likely a high S profile. High S's are described as being *deliberate, persistent, attentive, patient, humble, sincere, accommodating,* and *collaborative.* High S's accelerate their success when they are performing predictable work in a stable social environment. Let's look at the behavioral assets and liabilities of S sales professionals.

Behavioral assets that accelerate their selling success include:

- ☺ Listening attentively and empathetically
- ☺ Remaining loyal to people, teams, and companies
- ☺ Having a stabilizing effect on high I's
- ☺ Specializing in specific tasks or projects
- ☺ Remaining poised and patient, even under challenging circumstances

High S's accelerate their success by their naturally occurring strengths in each of the three phases of the Gap Analysis Sales Model ©:

> During the ASSESSMENT phase, S's are gifted in the art of active listening. In fact, they are the best listeners of all four profile groups, hearing both the verbally and non-verbally communicated message. They are also known for their empathy skills, which leaves clients feeling heard, understood, respected, and appreciated.

> During the PRESENTATION phase, S's are effective at keeping things conversational. They have a very low-pressure sales approach that places the client's needs ahead of their own. As a result they build trust easily.

> During the NEGOTIATION phase, S's are efficient at generating "fair" solutions. They will not sacrifice a relationship to achieve a self-serving outcome. They are naturally very collaborative and would rather join forces than oppose them. High S's are also very skilled at tuning into subtle, non-verbal communication and interpreting its meaning.

High S's make wonderful sales professionals, especially when engaged in activities that align with their naturally patient sales profile.

---

**ASSESSMENT TIP:**

High S's make wonderful sales professionals, especially when engaged in activities that align with their naturally patient sales profile.

---

Just as S's have naturally occurring behavioral assets that accelerate their success, so too do they have liabilities that can decelerate their success. These include:

☹ Resisting personal and professional change
☹ Harboring grudges toward others
☹ Failing to question the status quo
☹ Failing to be proactive when the situation demands it
☹ Being unwilling to confront others face to face

Due to their nature, S's are reluctant to step out of their comfort zone and embrace changes within their business environment. They are more comfortable in places, and with people, that have proven to be safe, and reliable.

## The Pure S

There are four primary S profiles within this group. The first is the "Pure S," known for having a patient, caring, and deliberate nature. Nicole Kidman, Wayne Dyer, and singer/ songwriter Sarah McLachlan are all believed to be members of this profile group.

Here are the behavioral pairings of this profile group and the corresponding value these combinations bring to a specific role or team.

## The SD

If your profile is primary S with secondary D, then you are often referred to as the "Deliberate Driver." Your greatest asset is your ability to apply your natural tenacity toward task completion or goal attainment. This behavioral pairing combines *deliberateness* and *dependability* with *assertiveness* and *directness*. Michael Jordan, Wayne Gretzky, and Roger Federer are believed to share this behavioral pairing.

In a team environment you are known as the "go to person" when it comes to applying tenacious efforts to achieve a specific and tangible outcome, like becoming the number one basketball, hockey, or tennis player in the world.

## The SI

If your profile is primary **S** with secondary **I** you are known as the "Stabilizer." This behavioral pairing combines *deliberateness* and *dependability* with *friendliness* and *persuasiveness*. This individual is particularly effective when working within a structured work environment. If this is your profile you are an effective listener and people trust that you will do what you say. People like Carrie Underwood, Tom Hanks, and Jennifer Aniston are thought to be members of this profile group.

In a team environment you are known as the "go to person" when the team needs to establish trust and manage the on-going client relationship.

## The SC

And finally the **SC** profile. This profile, known as the "Specialist," combines the qualities of *dependability* and *deliberateness* with an adherence to *policy* and *procedure*. The medical, dental and legal professions are well represented by members of this profile group. Well-known people like director Steven Spielberg, and airline pilot Chelsea "Sully" Sullenberger, who safely and calmly landed an Airbus A320 onto the Hudson River, are believed to share this behavioral pairing. If this is your profile, you are naturally effective at performing to a consistent and acceptable work standard, even in the face of challenging circumstances.

In a team environment you are the "go to person" when it comes time to setting the team up with systems for success.

If you have either of these high **S** sales profiles, recognize that you bring uniquely specific strengths to your profession and value to your team. Ensure that you direct your work efforts toward those activities that are supported by your naturally occurring behavioral strengths.

---

### ASSESSMENT ACTION PLAN

O━▪INSIGHTS:

Know that high S sales professionals accelerate their success when they are performing predictable work in a stable, low-pressure environment.

O━▪SKILLS:

Apply the principles of DISC to help you structure your business activities to align with your Steadiness level.

---

> *"Beware of the person who can't be bothered*
> *by the details."*
> – William Feather

# EVERYTHING'S IN ORDER!

### The GAP

Some high Compliance sales professionals fail to recognize the inherent strengths and limitations of their sales profile and subsequently neglect to align their business accordingly.

### The BRIDGE

Do you get frustrated with others who buck policy or bypass procedure? Do you like to double-check your work to ensure accuracy? Do you require a lot of information before you make a purchase decision and sometimes obsess over the details? When you do buy a piece of electronics, do you fill out the warranty cards or buy the extended warranty to protect your investment? Are you adamant about paying your bills on time at the end of every month?

If your answer is "yes" to the majority of these statements then you have high Compliance tendencies. High C's are described as being *diplomatic, tactful, systematic, accurate, logical, reserved, exacting,* and *conservative*. They are all about **policy**.

Evidence confirms that high C's accelerate their success when they are working toward task completion on activities related to their subject matter expertise. Let's look at the behavioral assets and liabilities of high C sales professionals.

Behavioral assets that accelerate their selling success include:

- ☺ Following policy and procedure
- ☺ Communicating in a diplomatic manner

☺ Ensuring standards are met
☺ Operating in a controlled environment
☺ Delivering as promised

High C's accelerate their success by applying their natural occurring strengths in each of the three phases of the Gap Analysis Sales Model ©:

> During the ASSESSMENT phase, high C's are naturally skilled at listening for factual content. They are very methodical at uncovering their client's specific product/ service needs and are known for their ability to communicate with patience and diplomacy. Unlike S profiles, who are empathetic listeners, C's are attentive listeners, skilled in the art of hearing and interpreting relevant factual data.

> During the PRESENTATION phase, high C's are effective at delivering thorough and well-structured presentations. Although not known for their engaging delivery style or charismatic presence, they are effective when presenting on topics on which they are subject matter experts.

> During the NEGOTIATION phase, high C's are highly skilled at uncovering evidence to support their negotiating position. They are accurate and thorough in their research and in drafting enforceable agreements. C's don't like to make mistakes so they dot all their i's and cross all their t's. When encountering resistance they'll remain non-confrontational, preferring to work through problems using logic and reason as their guide.

High C's make highly competent sales professionals, and are especially effective when engaged in activities that align with their naturally analytical sales profile.

---

## ASSESSMENT TIP:

**High C's make highly competent
sales professionals, especially when
engaged in activities that align with
their naturally analytical sales profile.**

---

Just as C's have naturally occurring behavioral assets that
accelerate their success, so too do they have liabilities that can
decelerate their success. These include:

☹ Yielding a position to avoid confrontation
☹ Dismissing ideas that are not supported by logic
☹ Getting bogged down in excessive detail
☹ Failing to take action if no precedence is set
☹ Getting defensive when their findings are questioned

As with the other groups, there are four primary C profiles.

### The Pure C

The first is the "Pure C," who is highly analytical and
unemotional by nature. The Spock character from the original *Star
Trek* series is the epitome of a person with this particular profile.
There are very few publicly recognized members of this profile
group because popularity and recognition is not of interest to them.
"Pure C's" are more comfortable remaining anonymous and behind
the scenes.

Here are the behavioral pairings of the high C profile and the
corresponding value these combinations bring to a specific role and
team.

## The CD

If your profile is primary **C** with secondary **D** then your psychometric brand identity is known as the "Enforcer." This behavioral pairing adds the qualities of *assertiveness* and *directness* to your *logical* and *systematic* nature. Your greatest asset is your ability to apply standards, rules, and systems and ensure they are followed. Bill Gates, Mark Zuckerberg, and the late Steve Jobs are thought to be members of this profile group.

In a team environment you are known as the "go to person" when it comes to establishing systems and ensuring compliance.

## The CI

If your profile is primary **C** with secondary **I** then you are someone who is *accurate, detailed,* and *compliant* and at the same time *outgoing, gregarious,* and *charming.* It is the psychometric equivalent of a tax auditor with a great sense of humor. Although somewhat rare, those who do share this behavioral pairing are affectionately referred to as a "Systems Promoter." If this is you then you're known to have a naturally strong ability to promote conceptual ideas using logic and reason.

In a team environment you are the "go to person" when it comes to managing systems.

## The CS

If your profile is primarily **C** and secondary **S** then you are referred to as the "Technical Analyst." You have a strong ability to maintain high standards and follow policy and procedures. This behavioral pairing combines *accuracy* and *logic* with *deliberateness* and *consistency.* Members of this profile group are thought to include John McCain, Al Gore, and environmental steward David Suzuki.

In a team environment you are the "go to person" when it comes time to communicating the technical aspects of a sophisticated product/ service offering.

If you have either of these high C sales profiles, recognize that you bring uniquely specific strengths to your profession and value to your team. Ensure that you direct your work efforts toward those activities that are supported by your naturally occurring behavioral strengths.

---

### ASSESSMENT ACTION PLAN

---

**○━►INSIGHTS:**

Know that high **C** sales professionals accelerate their success when they are working toward task completion on activities related to their subject matter expertise.

**○━►SKILLS:**

Apply the principles of **DISC** to help you structure your business activities to align with your Compliance level.

~Chapter Two~

# Recognizing Your Client's Buying Style

*Accelerate your selling success by profiling your clients to establish their unique decision-making needs.*

*"We don't see things as they are; we see things as we are."*
– Anais Nin

> *"A client's 'buyer profile' can be identified by anyone willing to look for the signs and able to interpret their meaning."*
> – Gerald G. Clerx

# WHAT IS MY CLIENT'S BUYER PROFILE?

## The GAP

Most sales professionals don't consider the preferred buying style (buyer profile) of their prospective client and subsequently fail to understand his/ her unique decision-making needs.

## The BRIDGE

Just as a person's behavioral profile impacts how he/ she sells, so too does it impact how he /she prefers to buy. Knowing a client's buyer profile is imperative if you are to design and deliver a presentation that aligns accordingly.

---

### ASSESSMENT TIP:

Knowing a client's buyer profile is
imperative if you are to design
and deliver a presentation
that aligns accordingly.

---

Assessing a client's buyer profile is not as difficult as you might think. In fact, behavioral clues are visible for all to see; however, they will only have meaning for those who know how to interpret its meaning. When you get good at this you can assess profiles in a very short period of time, sometimes instantly.

A client's buyer profile will provide you with insights into exactly what he or she needs to *see, hear,* and *experience* to fully support a favorable buying decision. The quickest way to identify a client's profile is to observe the following *verbal, vocal,* and *visual* communication patterns:

## Verbal Identifiers

When observing verbal patterns, pay attention to the types of *words* and *phrases* being used as well as the types of *questions* asked. Different profile groups rely on certain words and phrases more heavily and place greater emphasis on specific types of information.

---

### ASSESSMENT TIP:

When observing verbal patterns, pay attention to the types of *words* and *phrases* being used as well as the *questions* asked.

---

## Vocal Identifiers

When observing vocal communication patterns, pay attention to your client's *pace, tone,* and *volume.* Vocal patterns are a reflection of internal processing preferences.

Observing your client's vocal patterns will also help you narrow down his/ her buyer profile. For instance: two profile groups speak quicker than the norm and two slower; two use a more businesslike tone and two a more casual tone; two speak at a louder volume and two softer. Through a process of elimination, you can narrow down a client's buyer profile just by paying attention to his/ her vocal communication patterns.

## Visual Identifiers

When observing visual patterns, focus in on *body posture, hand gestures,* and *facial expressions*. It is estimated that body language accounts for 57 percent of the communicated message, so pay close attention to what is being conveyed visually.

---

### ASSESSMENT TIP:

**It is estimated that body language accounts for 57 percent of the communicated message, so pay close attention to what is being conveyed visually.**

---

The reason why most sales professionals fail to recognize their client's buyer profile is because they're engaged in "self-centric" rather than "client-centric" behavior. They're more concerned with what they're saying and how they're appearing than they are on the prospective client.

When profiling your client, however, be sure to base your assessment on more than just one clue. Use a "clustering technique" instead by making multiple observations over a period of a few minutes, to ensure the greatest degree of accuracy.

The next time you meet a new client, tune in verbally by listening to the *words* and *phrases* used and the types of *questions* asked. Tune in vocally to *tone, pace,* and *volume* and finally tune in visually by observing *body posture, hand gestures,* and *facial expressions*. A lot can be learned by paying attention to your client's communication patterns.

But keep in mind, observation is only the first step; interpretation is the second. In the following four acceleration strategies, you'll learn how to identify each of the four buyer profiles by interpreting their respective communication patterns.

---

## ASSESSMENT ACTION PLAN

---

**O——INSIGHTS:**

Know that your prospective client is constantly exposing his/ her buyer profile *verbally, vocally,* and *visually,* and that you will be able to recognize it in less than two minutes once you know what to look for.

**O——SKILLS:**

Apply a clustering technique to focus on what your client is saying (verbal) and how she is saying it (vocal and visual) to help you identify his/ her buyer profile.

**O——RESOURCES:**

Refer to the *Client Assessment Tool* to determine your client's buyer profile. Go to www.theGAPanalysis.com and click on "Resources" page to learn more.

> *"Do not go where the path may lead,*
> *go instead where there is no path and leave a trail."*
> – Ralph Waldo Emerson

# What's the Bottom Line?

### The GAP

Most sales professionals fail to recognize a high **D** client and as a result, neglect to tailor their sales presentation to align with his unique decision-making needs.

### The BRIDGE

If you've ever had a client interrupt your presentation by asking "What's the bottom line?" or by saying "Cut to the chase," or by tapping fingers when wanting you to pick up the pace? If you've ever had a client take your proposal from your hands and turn straight to the last page to check out how much it's going to cost or how much he stands to make in the transaction then you've been in the presence of a high **D** client.

Remember, Dominance is a reflection of a person's response to **power**. High **D**'s are *actively paced* and *task focused*, which means they like to move quickly toward a specific and tangible result.

Spotting a **D** is an easy thing to do if you know what identifiers to look for. Here are some of the *verbal, vocal* and *visual* identifiers of the high **D** client:

### Verbal Identifiers

Let's start with the words and phrases that you'll hear expressed more frequently by members of this profile group. Words such as *success, results, priority access, quickly, outcome, driven, aggressive, leadership, top dollar, top producer, assert,* and *overcome* are all prominent in the high **D** vocabulary. Some of their more common phrases include:

*Cut to the chase!*

*Get to the point!*

*You've got to be kidding me!*

*Quit wasting my time!*

*Let's get down to business!*

*Skip the small talk!*

and, in Donald Trump's case, *YOU'RE FIRED!*

A client's buyer profile can also be determined by listening to the types of questions asked. Since **D**'s *fear failure* and *desire quick results*, the bulk of their questions will seek to either alleviate their fears or confirm the realization of their desires. For example, during the ASSESSMENT phase a high **D** client might ask:

*How long is this going to take?*

*What do you have for me?*

*What's your fee and how do you justify it?*

*What is the upside potential?*

*How quickly can you move on this?*

The purpose of a **D**'s questions is to elicit the essential information required to make a quick decision leading to a tangible outcome.

## Vocal Identifiers

A **D** client's buyer profile can also be recognized by his/ her vocal *pace*, *tone*, and *volume*.

Since they are in the active behavior quadrant, their vocal *pace* moves along at a faster clip when compared to the norm. They don't necessarily speak quicker but they do get to the point quicker, as reflected in their bottom line-oriented questioning style.

Vocally, D's have a *tone* that is more businesslike and matter-of-fact than the norm. Indeed, they are the most matter-of-fact and businesslike of all four profile groups.

The *volume* of their voice covers a wide dynamic range, from quiet and controlled to loud and assertive. When frustrated, the D's vocal *volume* can rise sharply with little or no warning.

## Behavioral Identifiers - Visual

High D's visual communication patterns can be observed through their *body posture*, *hand gestures,* and *facial expressions.*

Visually, a high D's body posture is more rigid than those in the other profile groups. They tend to stand and sit in a more upright position and lean in when expressing their opinions or showing interest in your product/ service offering.

Their more assertive nature can also be observed in the way they point toward those things that interest them and the way they pound their index finger into the table to ensure their point is made. Peaking the fingertips in an *"I'm in control here"* way is another classic D hand gesture. While other buyer profiles use more expansive and/ or open-palmed hand gestures, D gesturing is more directional and out in front.

A handshake from a high D is another strong clue. It will almost always involve a firm grip accompanied by direct eye contact. If you want to test your client's level of Dominance, simply maintain eye contact. A D profile will hold eye contact longer than the other profile groups. In some cases you'll receive a handshake that begins vertically and ends up with them turning your hand into a horizontal position, with theirs on top. This is a subtle way in which some D's test your response to assertive behavior. If they encounter physical resistance during the greeting, they'll know to expect verbal resistance during the negotiation.

Facial expressions account for the balance of behavioral identifiers. The D's forehead often supports a furrowed brow, especially when questioning the source of your information. The eyes are usually fixed in an intense gaze and smiles are not easily forthcoming. If a smile is elicited during the sales cycle, it will likely be short-lived, so as not to encourage small talk or to infer flexibility.

Another way to obtain clues into your client's psychometric profile is by noticing their workplace. A high **D**'s work environment is often bold, clean, and efficient and the office walls adorned with awards to showcase personal accomplishments.

The **D**'s three favorite colors are black, dark black, and midnight black. Actually it's black, navy, and charcoal grey, which are the traditional power colors in our society. The vast majority of automobiles targeted toward this buyer group come in these three primary color choices. If this profile group had a theme song it would be "I Did It My Way," sung by high **D** alumni, Frank Sinatra.

High **D**'s are easy to spot, straight to the point, and quick to partner with sales professionals who understand their unique needs and adapt accordingly.

---

### ASSESSMENT TIP:

**High D's are easy to spot and
quick to partner with sales
professionals who understand their
unique needs and adapt accordingly.**

---

When you first meet with a prospective client, pay close attention to his level of Dominance. Knowing the client's buyer profile is an important piece of the sales puzzle because, as you will discover in chapter five, presenting your product/ service solution to a high **D** client looks and sounds nothing like delivering a presentation to members of the other profile groups.

In the next Acceleration Strategy, you'll learn how to recognize a client with a high Influence profile.

---

## ASSESSMENT ACTION PLAN

---

**○━INSIGHTS:**

Know that your client is always exposing his/ her Dominance level through *verbal*, *vocal*, and *visual* communication patterns.

**○━SKILLS:**

Apply observation skills to detect:

- Language that reflects an *active pace* and *task focus*.

- Vocal qualities that include a *faster pace*, *business tone*, and *louder volume*.

- Body language that includes an *erect posture*, *assertive hand gestures*, and more *intense facial expressions*.

# CAN I GET IT IN RED?

## The GAP

Most sales professionals fail to recognize a high **I** client and as a result, neglect to tailor their sales presentation to align with her unique decision-making needs.

## The BRIDGE

If you've ever met a client who loved to talk, or if you've ever shown up late for an appointment and your client showed up later, or if you've ever met someone who gave you a hearty double-handed, triple-pumping handshake accompanied by a broad, friendly grin then you've been in the presence of a high Influence client.

Remember, Influence is a reflection of a person's response to **people**. High **I**'s are *actively paced* and *socially focused*, which means they like to move enthusiastically toward the development of the relationship. The product/ service outcome is almost secondary to the engagement process.

Here are some of the *verbal*, *vocal*, and *visual* identifiers of the high **I** client:

## Verbal Identifiers

Verbal identifiers include words and phrases that are more descriptive and colorful by nature. Ask a high **I** how she is doing and you will likely get a response such as *I'm excellent, Couldn't be better*! or perhaps even *Outstanding*! The responses of *I'm fine* or *I'm OK* are not common amongst this profile group, even if she is feeling under the weather. Some favored phrases reflective of this group's enthusiastic and optimistic nature include:

*No worries!*

*Not a problem!*

*Great to finally meet you!*

*How the heck are you!*

*Now where were we?*

*Where did the day go?* And

*Sorry I'm late!* (I's have a far more elastic concept of time than the other profile groups)

The greatest fear of the high I is *loss of influence*, and the greatest desire is for *recognition and acceptance*. These two underlying motivators are reflected in the often personally directed questions a high I client may ask you, especially during the ASSESSMENT phase. These questions may include:

*So how long have you been selling?*

*How do you like the business?*

*Which one of these is **your** favorite?*

*What do **you** recommend we should do?*

*Are you doing anything later this week?*

It's important to note that high I's are relationship driven, so they inherently seek to find commonality and develop relationships whenever and wherever the opportunity avails itself. In many cases, short-term professional relationships can develop into long-term personal friendships.

## Vocal Identifiers

Now let's shift to vocal identifiers, beginning with *pace*. Of all four buyer profiles, high I's speak the fastest. In some cases they'll speak before fully thinking through the consequences of their words. *"I can't believe I just said that,"* or *"Did I just say that out loud?"* are classic recovery phrases for the high I. Virtually all feet ending up in the mouths of their owner belong to members of this particular profile group.

Regarding vocal *tone*, I's are far less businesslike than their **D** counterparts. Rather than *"Let's get down to business,"* it's more like *"Tell me a little about yourself"* or better yet, *"Let me tell you a little about myself."* They laugh more than the other profile groups and the higher the **I**, the heartier the laugh.

Vocal *volume* for high I's is, on average, louder than the norm. Other profile groups may find this characteristic to be a source of annoyance, especially the more passive Steadiness and Compliance profiles.

## Visual Identifiers

Visually, **I** clients are easy to spot. Their enthusiastic persona is often expressed through brighter colors and trendier clothes adorned with more plentiful accessories. Favored colors include red, yellow and other more cheerful hues.

A high **I**'s body language is looser and more open than their **D** counterparts. Their posture is flexible and they tend to lean toward those things that interest them. They get closer, quicker than other buyer profiles, and they are far more comfortable sharing their space, especially with fellow **I**'s. Physical contact is far more prevalent between members of this profile group. Receiving a touch to the top of the hand or back of the elbow is not uncommon while engaged in conversation with the high **I**.

Their hand gestures are more expansive and more animated than most others. Whereas **D**'s tend to limit their gestures to a 45-degree range directly in front, **I**'s express themselves with a full 180-degree range of motion. They'll often exaggerate their gestures to make a point (i.e. the size of the fish actually caught is rarely the size of the fish they claim they caught).

Receiving a handshake from a high **I** can also be a unique experience, especially if you are not a member of this profile group. A double-pumping shake accompanied by a broad smile and enthusiastic greeting is the norm. Heck, you may even receive the infamous double-handed, double-pumping handshake, which indicates of a high level of personal acceptance.

However, be wary of the double-handed, *triple-pumping* handshake. If you get one of these from a high I client leave the area immediately—as he or she likely has bigger plans for you.

High I's are, by far, the most animated of all four profile groups. Broader smiles and more extreme reactions are the norm. When listening, they nod their head in an enthusiastic and encouraging way (even if they haven't the foggiest idea of what you're talking about). This group can give the outward appearance of being fully engrossed in your story while mentally sipping a margarita on some sunny tropical beach.

The I's office environment is brighter and bolder than the other profile groups; however, it will likely appear to be a little on the chaotic side. Photographs and pictures are often self-directed, showcasing unique personal experiences or adventures. Their office is set up to be more conducive for socializing than for work, and the desk will most likely be facing the door to facilitate dialogue with those passing by.

If the high I had a theme song, it would be "Don't Worry, Be Happy." These lyrics represent their basic philosophical approach to life. Ahh, high I's—you've got to love them! I mean that seriously, **you've got to**. It's a behavioral expectation I's have from all their acquaintances.

High I's are easy to spot and eager to partner with sales professionals who understand their unique needs and adapt accordingly.

---

### ASSESSMENT TIP:

**High I's are easy to spot, and eager to partner with sales professionals who understand their unique needs and adapt accordingly.**

---

So when you meet a prospective client, pay attention to his/her level of Influence. As you'll discover in chapter five; presenting your product/ service solution to a high **I** client looks and sounds nothing like delivering a presentation to members of any other profile group.

In the next Acceleration Strategy, you will learn how to identify high Steadiness clients by observing their unique *verbal*, *vocal*, and *visual* behavioral patterns.

---

### ASSESSMENT ACTION PLAN

---

**O——INSIGHTS:**

**Know** that your client is always exposing his/ her Influence level through *verbal*, *vocal* and *visual* communication patterns.

**O——SKILLS:**

**Apply** observation skills to detect:

- Language that reflects an *active pace* and *social focus*.

- Vocal qualities that include a *faster pace*, *friendlier tone*, and *louder volume*.

- Body language that includes a more *casual posture* with *animated gestures* and *facial expressions*.

# WHO ELSE HAS BOUGHT ONE?

## The GAP

Most sales professionals fail to recognize a high S client and as a result, neglect to tailor their sales presentation to align with her unique decision-making needs.

## The BRIDGE

If you've ever had a client greet you with a warm smile and a gentle handshake and follow up by asking questions and listening patiently to your responses. Or if you've ever had a client that calmed you down and put you immediately at ease, then you've interacted with a high S.

Remember, Steadiness is a reflection of a person's response to pace. High S's are *passively paced* and *socially focused*, which means that they move deliberately toward an understanding of people and processes. Spotting them is an easy thing to do if you know what to listen and look for. Here are some of the *verbal*, *vocal*, and *visual* clues offered up by the high S profile.

## Verbal Identifiers

Verbally, high S's communicate with a strong reliance on words such as *together*, *we've*, and *let's*. It's called the language of collaboration and they speak it fluently. Commonly used high S phrases include:

*That seems fair.*

*I'll go along with that.*

*It is a pleasure to meet you.*
*Thank you so much for coming.*
*Wouldn't you agree?*
*I'm just looking, thank you.*

Now reflect on these phrases for a moment. You just won't hear these statements made by a high **D** client.

The high **S**'s greatest fear is *loss of stability*, and his/ her great desire is for *safety and security*; therefore the questions asked will reflect these two underlying motivators. During the ASSESSMENT phase, an **S** client might ask:

*Who will be involved in this sale or project?*
*What are their respective roles?*
*Who is my contact person?*
*Can you provide me some timelines?*
*Who else have you worked with?*
*Do you have any references?*
*Can I return it if I am not happy?*
*Do you guarantee your work?*

## Vocal Identifiers

Vocally, high **S**'s speak at a slower and more *deliberate pace* than the norm. They are in no hurry and their vocal pace reflects this more relaxed conversational style, which can be a source of frustration for the *actively paced* **D** and **I** sales professionals.

Regarding vocal *tone*, the **S** is less businesslike than the high **D** but more businesslike than the high **I**. Once trust has been established, the high **S** warms up considerably.

A high **S**'s vocal *volume* is much softer than that of the previous two profile groups. They exhibit more patience than others, and their pauses are longer as they give more thought-*full* consideration to their responses.

## Visual Identifiers

Visually, S profiles have a more relaxed posture. They spend more time in a listening mode and will keep their distance until trust has been earned. You can often observe them leaning back, reflecting upon the information presented.

Their hand gestures are gentler and less expansive than those with high Dominance and Influence profiles. Instead of pointing gestures, they rely more on open-palmed and rolling hand gestures.

A high S handshake is warm, friendly, and the least firm of the four profile groups overall. In some cases the hand is extended without any firmness to their grip whatsoever (note: this can also reflect a culturally inherited mannerism). High S's do not feel the need to deliver an assertive or overly enthusiastic greeting. It's not what they're about!

Facial expressions during initial greetings can best be described as warm and inviting. They convey acceptance with a relaxed smile and reassuring eyes. Be assured, however, that their pleasant demeanor will shift if they feel threatened or mislead.

The high S dresses more for comfort than for prestige or impact. Sweaters, loose-fitting clothes, and soft-soled shoes are more the norm for this profile group. This is not to say that they will always be casually attired, it's just more within their comfort zone.

Their office often reflects this desire for comfort with images of family and loved ones displayed throughout. Their personal space will have a cozier and warmer feel than the other profile groups, with preferred colors being earth tones such as white, beige, and greens.

If the high S had a theme song it would be, "That's What Friends Are For"; after all, the high S's identity is strongly linked to the quality of his/ her personal and professional relationships.

High S clients are easy to spot and secure in partnering with sales professionals who understand their unique needs and adapt accordingly.

---

## ASSESSMENT TIP:

**High S clients are easy to spot and
secure in partnering with sales
professionals who understand their
unique needs and adapt accordingly.**

---

Pay attention to your client's level of Steadiness. As you'll discover in chapter five, presenting your product/ service solution to a high S client looks and sounds nothing like presenting to members of the other profile groups.

In the next Acceleration Strategy, you will learn how to recognize a high Compliance client.

---

## ASSESSMENT ACTION PLAN

---

**O——INSIGHTS:**

Know that your client is always expressing his/ her Steadiness level through *verbal*, *vocal*, and *visual* communication patterns.

**O——SKILLS:**

Apply observation skills to detect:

- Language that reflects a *passive pace* and *social focus*.

- Vocal qualities that include a *slower pace*, *friendlier tone* and *softer volume*.

- Body language that includes a *relaxed posture*, *softer hand gestures*, and *warmer facial expressions*.

> *"Facts are stubborn things."*
> – Ronald Reagan

# Do You Have Any Specs?

### The GAP

Most sales professionals fail to recognize a high **C** client and as a result, neglect to tailor their sales presentations to align with his unique decision-making needs.

### The BRIDGE

If you've ever had a client ask more than the usual amount of questions and require a lot of evidence to support a buying decision, or if the client spoke painfully slow by your standards, or had a greater depth and breadth of knowledge of your competitors' offering than you did, then you've interacted with a high **C**.

Remember, Compliance is a reflection of a person's response to **policy**. High C's are *passively paced* and *task focused*, which means they move methodically toward a comprehensive understanding of the situation. Spotting a high **C** is an easy thing to do if you know what to listen and look for. Here are some of the *verbal, vocal,* and *visual* clues offered up by members of this profile group.

### Verbal Identifiers

High C's are heavily reliant on words that are both qualitative and quantitative. Words like; *assessment, comprehensive, historical analysis, proof, assurances,* and *guarantees* are frequently relied upon to communicate ideas and opinions. Common high C phrases include:

> *It seems to me.*
> *That sounds <u>reasonable</u>.*
> *I'll <u>consider</u> that.*

*Let me think it over.*
*Leave it with me.*

Consider the words that are underlined: *reasonable* (reason able), *consider* and *think*. This is the left-brained and linear dialogue of the high Compliance client, and it is as distinct a language as English is from French.

Remember, the high C's greatest fear is *making a mistake*, and his/ her greatest desire is for *full and accurate disclosure*. These underlying motivators are evidenced by the types of questions high C's ask, which are intended to gather the information necessary to support their logical decision-making needs.

During your interaction with a high C, he or she might ask:
*How did you arrive at these figures?*
*Is your commission negotiable?*
*Why is your competition offering this same service at half your fee?*
*What are the operating costs of this product?*
*Who are the manufacturers and where are they based?*
*Do you have any updated spec sheets?*
*Are you prepared to put up any assurances or guarantees?*

## Vocal Identifiers

High C's vocal *pace* matches their information processing preference, which tends to be much slower than the norm. They are not quick to render decisions, which can be a great source of frustration for the faster paced high D's and I's.

Their vocal *tone* is the most formal of all profile groups and can be recognized by a conservative, businesslike, and often monotone quality. Listening to a high C talk for a long period of time is a real test to the attention span of the faster paced and more social profile groups.

Their vocal *volume* is lower than others', and in some cases you may have to lean in and strain to hear their words.

## Visual Identifiers

The body posture of the high **C** is less open than the more social **I**'s and **S**'s. In a sales environment the high **C** prefers to keep a distance, while carefully considering the information being presented.

Their hand gestures are far less expansive or expressive than in the other profile groups, with arms remaining tighter to their bodies. Their handshake is conservative and can be recognized by a firm grip without the intense and enduring eye contact of the high **D**.

High **C**'s facial expressions are the least animated of the four profile groups. It's not uncommon for the high **C** to spend the full duration of your presentation focusing on your content rather than on you. A lengthy period of reflection should be anticipated before a decision is rendered.

Physically, the appearance of high **C**'s is more conservative than the other profile groups. Rather than dressing for impact, trend consciousness or comfort, they dress to reflect professionalism.

You can expect their office environment to be tidy and symmetrical. Pictures will be hung with precision and credentials will be prominently displayed as a show of professional competence. Preferred colors include the more conservative tones of browns, navy blues, and grey.

High **C**'s are detail-oriented and confident in partnering with sales professionals who understand their unique needs and adapt accordingly.

---

### ASSESSMENT TIP:

High **C**'s are detail-oriented and confident in partnering with sales professionals who understand their unique needs and adapt accordingly.

---

Pay close attention to your client's level of Compliance. As you'll discover in chapter five; presenting your product/ service solution to a high C client looks and sounds nothing like delivering a presentation to the other buyer profiles.

So there you have it: the verbal, vocal, and visual identifiers of the four profile groups. By following these guidelines, you should be able to identify the buyer profile of your next client within the first few minutes of your initial meeting.

However, keep in mind that knowing your client's buyer profile is only one piece of a two-piece puzzle. In PART II of this book, you'll discover how to take this behavioral awareness and use it to shape your presentation and tailor its delivery. You'll discover what to say and why, and how to say it in a way that supports the client's unique decision-making needs.

---

### ASSESSMENT ACTION PLAN

---

**O—►INSIGHTS:**

Know that your client is always exposing his/ her Compliance level through *verbal*, *vocal*, and *visual* communication patterns.

**O—►SKILLS:**

Apply observation skills to detect:

- Language that reflects a *passive pace* and *task focus*.

- Vocal qualities that includes a *slower pace, businesslike tone* and *softer volume*.

- Body language that includes a more *defensive posture, less animated gestures*, and *more reserved facial expressions*.

THE **ASSESSMENT** PHASE

~Chapter Three~

# Assessing Your Client's Gap

*Accelerate your selling success by isolating your client's product/ service gap.*

൭

*"Seek first to understand, then to be understood."*
– Stephen Covey

> *"If your clients don't have confidence in your diagnosis, they won't have confidence in your prescription."*
> – Gerald G. Clerx

# SEEK FIRST TO UNDERSTAND

**The GAP**

Most sales professionals build their presentations on the foundation of an inconclusive assessment and by doing so, fail to demonstrate their product/ service offering to be an effective solution to the client problem.

**The BRIDGE**

In chapter two I introduced you to a **DISC**-based assessment strategy to help you identify the behavioral profile of your client.

In addition to profiling your client, the other purpose of the ASSESSMENT phase is to isolate the gap between where your client is and where he/ she wants to be.

---

ASSESSMENT TIP:

The other purpose of the ASSESSMENT
phase is to isolate the gap between
where your client is and where
he/ she wants to be.

---

These reference points form the foundation upon which every sales presentation is built—a road map, if you will, complete with a clearly defined departure point and arrival destination. Once these are known, the sales person's role is to simply bridge that gap with the best product/ service solution available.

Unfortunately, this isn't the approach most sales professionals take—instead they prescribe a solution without having fully diagnosed the problem. It is the equivalent of a seamstress tailoring a suit without knowing the wearer's measurements or intended usage. The finished product might look fabulous but not fit worth a darn or serve any practical purpose.

As a success-minded sales professional, your primary objective should be to fully and accurately uncover your client's gap. Depending on the type of product you sell or service you promote, there could be up to fifty pieces of information required to accurately establish these two reference points.

---

### ASSESSMENT TIP:

Depending on the type of product
you sell or service you promote,
there could be up to fifty pieces
of information required to accurately
establish these two reference points.

---

Now I'm not suggesting that you corner a client and fire off fifty rounds of high velocity questions; however, I am suggesting that you engage them in a fact-finding dialogue to gather as much information as possible before you make your recommendations.

Also bear in mind that the questioning approach you employ should be a reflection of your client's buyer profile. Let's stop for a minute and test your **DISC** knowledge here. Which two profile groups will not tolerate a lengthy questioning strategy? ..................... You'd be right if you identified the high **D**'s and

I's. The **D**'s don't have the time and the **I**'s don't have the attention span. Now don't get me wrong, you'll still require the information; however, you might have to bridge the information gaps via a third party source.

On the other hand, high **S**'s and high **C**'s will respond far more favorably to a comprehensive questioning strategy. Why? Because they're in no hurry to make a decision! In fact, their respective key motivators—a *desire* for safety and a *fear* of making a mistake—both align favorably with a sales professional who is willing to take the time up front to ask the right questions that ensure a safe and mistake-free outcome.

A secondary benefit of conducting a comprehensive assessment is the opportunity to discover that your client's *desired* reality is not a realistic reflection of what his/ her *current* financial ability will reasonably accommodate. If this is the case, you have one of two options:

1. Get your client to change his/ her *desired* reality, and if they won't
2. Refer your client to the competition—after all, **your** time is a valuable resource.

Understand that an inconclusive assessment causes everyone to lose. You lose, the client loses, and so too does anyone else who has time or money invested in the transaction.

On the flip side, a comprehensive assessment almost always guarantees you a successful outcome. It allows you to show fewer, more selectively defined products and it makes it easier for your client to say, "yes" to your recommendation. And because your client will recognize you as a competent and skilled professional, he or she will feel less inclined to request a fee concession or service discount as a condition of purchase.

In my experience, the true testament to a sales professional's level of competence can be traced back to the questions he or she asks (or fails to ask) and their willingness to fully hear the response. Sales professionals who are "self-motivated" are selective listeners, hearing only that which furthers their own personal agenda. On the other hand, sales professionals who ask meaningful questions and listen fully to the answer before responding demonstrate a "client-centric" focus and are more apt to secure a favorable outcome. After all, a salesperson that listens fully before speaking fulfills two fundamental human needs: *to feel heard* and *to be understood*.

---

### ASSESSMENT TIP:

A sales professional who listens fully before speaking fulfills two fundamental human needs: *to feel heard* and *to be understood*.

---

Sales professionals who are attentive and empathetic listeners are in high demand and short supply.

Seek First to Understand

---

### ASSESSMENT ACTION PLAN

---

**O━━▸INSIGHTS:**

    **Know** that the single biggest reason why a sales presentation fails is because it was built on the foundation of a weak assessment.

**O━━▸SKILLS:**

    **Apply** a comprehensive questioning strategy that effectively isolates your client's product/ service gap.

**O━━▸RESOURCES:**

    **Refer** to the following two Acceleration Strategies as your resources to uncover your prospect's *current reality condition* and *desired reality outcome*.

> *"If you don't know where you're going,*
> *any road will take you there."*
> – Yogi Berra

# WHERE ARE YOU GOING?

## The GAP

The quote above summarizes why many sales presentations fail: because most sales professionals begin their sales journey without having the foggiest idea of where they are going. They just start driving, hoping to stumble upon the right road that takes them to their client's desired destination.

## The BRIDGE

The primary objective of the ASSESSMENT phase is to get your client to clearly articulate his/ her desired outcome. Clarity of vision is a powerful thing. When clients are clear of exactly what they want, what they want tends to show up for them. You are far better off working with clients who can describe with absolute certainty what they're looking for, because they'll be able to recognize it when you deliver it.

---

### ASSESSMENT TIP:

Clarity of vision is a powerful thing.
When clients are clear of exactly
what they want, what they want
tends to show up for them.

---

Your client's desired reality has been fully defined when you have certainty on three decision-making criteria: *Satisfiers, Justifiers* and *Motivators*.

## Satisfiers

Satisfiers represent what the client needs to have included in your product/ service offering. Depending on the product type, these needs could include:

- *Design needs,* which include the elements of product shape and/ or layout.
- *Material needs,* which include product construction type and texture.
- *Aesthetic needs,* which include product color and appearance.
- *Expansion needs,* which include product integration and compatibility features.
- *Functionality needs,* which include product ease of use and accessibility.
- *Economic needs,* which include product price, operating costs and maintenance costs.
- *Timing needs,* which include closing dates and delivery time frames.
- *Flexibility needs,* which include the ability to change or modify the product/ service offering.

## Justifiers

Justifiers are represented by what the client needs to know to support a purchase decision. This information is necessary to support the logical side of the decision-making brain. Understanding your client's **DISC** profile will provide you with a great deal of information into the type of information required. **D** and **C** profiles are highly logical and linear in their decision-making process; therefore, they'll want tangible evidence to support their purchase decision.

High **D** clients prefer a factual overview, while **C**'s prefer full disclosure, including all relevant facts, figures, statistics, and case studies. **I**'s and **S**'s are less reliant on factual evidence and instead prefer third party testimonials which they find more personal.

## Motivators

Motivators are represented by what your client needs to feel in order to support a purchase decision.

Key motivators can be elicited by asking probing questions such as, "Why is that important to you?" or "What will that give you"? The client's underlying key motivator will likely be uncovered by one of these probing questions. For instance, a need to drive a brightly colored vehicle or live in a trendy part of town might be inspired by a desire to feel more youthful or attractive to others.

*Desires* represent "moving toward" motivators and accelerate favorable buying decisions. Some of the more common desire-based motivators include:

- A *desire* to grow intellectually or spiritually
- A *desire* to look better
- A *desire* to feel better
- A *desire* to feel safer
- A *desire* for more convenience
- A *desire* to save time or become more productive
- A *desire* to live longer
- A *desire* to accumulate wealth
- A *desire* to be first
- A *desire* to be understood
- A *desire* for more meaning
- A *desire* for better relationships
- A *desire* for better performance
- A *desire* for recognition and acknowledgement
- A *desire* to feel informed

---

**ASSESSMENT TIP:**

**Motivators can be expressed as
either *fears* or *desires*.**

---

*Fears* represent "moving away from" motivators and can also act to support a buying decision if your client believes that your product/ service offering will take them away from that which they *fear*. Some of the more common *fears* that can motivate a favorable buying decision include:

- A *fear* of missing out
- A *fear* of losing
- A *fear* of change
- A *fear* of being trapped in an uncomfortable situation
- A *fear* of being rejected
- A *fear* of being judged critically
- A *fear* of not living up to a another's expectation
- A *fear* of failing
- A *fear* of making a mistake
- A *fear* of dying
- A *fear* of becoming a burden to others
- A *fear* of being hurt (physically or emotionally)
- A *fear* of hurting someone else

Home security systems, prescription drugs, breath mints, dandruff control shampoos, and cosmetics are a few of the products that have generated a lot of revenue by promising to move you away from what you fear.

---

### ASSESSMENT ACTION PLAN

---

O——◄INSIGHTS:

Know that you must get absolute certainty on your client's *desired reality* in order to bridge their product/ service gap.

O——◄SKILLS:

Apply a comprehensive questioning strategy that accurately assesses your client's *satisfiers*, *justifiers*, and *motivators*.

O——◄RESOURCES:

Refer to our *Gap Questioning Strategy* to assist you in isolating your client's *desired reality outcome*. Go to <u>www.theGAPanalysis.com</u> and click on "Resources" page to learn more.

# WHERE ARE YOU COMING FROM?

## The GAP

Most sales professionals neglect to ascertain their client's current reality conditions and by doing so, end up spinning their wheels with unqualified clients.

## The BRIDGE

Have you ever spent valuable time working with a client that you later discovered had neither the ability nor the motivation to take action on your product/ service offering? Frustrating, isn't it!

A comprehensive gap analysis questioning strategy is the best defense against a failed sales experience. The questions you ask ought to elicit the following current reality insights:

## Financial ability

These insights establish what the client is willing to pay or able to afford. Obviously, financial ability is only relevant on larger ticket items.

## Current Status

Current reality questions should also ascertain whether the client needs to *upgrade*, *replace* or *amend* his/ her existing product or service agreement. Depending on the complexity of the offering, your *current* reality questioning strategy could include the following questions:

- *Tell me about your current product/ service provider.*
- *When does your current product lease/service agreement expire?*
- *Who else is involved in the decision-making process?*
- *What criteria will you use to make your decision?*
- *What is your time frame for this project?*
- *What are your current usage patterns?*
- *What other considerations do you have?*

Obviously, the complexity of your questioning strategy should be a reflection of the complexity of your product/ service offering.

**Summary**

An effectively conducted assessment provides you with a complete understanding of the client and her product/ service gap. With these reference points known, you are in a position to move into the **second** phase of the Gap Analysis Sales Model ©, the PRESENTATION phase.

In the next part of this book, you'll learn how to take the information uncovered during the ASSESSMENT phase and use it to deliver the right solution in a way that aligns perfectly with the client's decision-making needs. You'll also discover a powerful whole-brain reasoning technique for structuring your message so that it *informs logically* and *inspires emotionally*. And finally, you will learn how to add impact to your message and enhance its long-term retention.

I will conclude this part of the book with a **DISC** based driving analogy that playfully summarizes the unique behavioral response patterns of each profile group:

*Question*: What do you get when four high **D**'s approach a four way stop sign?

*Answer*: **An accident!** Because they all assume the other drivers will yield to them.

*Question*: What do you get when four high **I**'s approach a four way stop sign?

*Answer*: **A party!** Any time you have four **I**'s together you have the makings of a spontaneous party.

*Question*: What do you get when four high **S**'s approach a four way stop sign?

*Answer*: **Gridlock!** Because they all patiently wave the other drivers through the intersection!

*Question*: What do you get when four high **C**'s approach a four way stop sign?

*Answer*: **They get out of the car, form a committee and redesign the intersection!** (Note: I'm convinced that is where the roundabout concept came from.)

---

### ASSESSMENT ACTION PLAN

---

**O—INSIGHTS:**

**Know** that you must get absolute clarity on your client's *current reality* situation if you are to successfully take your client to his/ her *desired reality* outcome.

**O—SKILLS:**

**Apply** a comprehensive questioning strategy that accurately establishes your client's *current reality* condition.

**O—RESOURCES:**

**Refer** to our *Gap Questioning Strategy* to assist you in isolating your client's *current reality* condition. Go to www.theGAPanalysis.com and click on "Resources" page to learn more.

## Excellence in Action – ASSESSMENT

**The GAP:**
The hotel industry is a highly competitive market in which your success is largely dependant upon the strength of your brand identity.

**The BRIDGE:**
Isadore (Izzy) Sharp was a masterful bridge builder. Well technically he built hotels ... the Four Seasons to be exact. The bridges he built, during his tenure as CEO, were not physical but rather experiential and each one of them transported his clients from a satisfactory hotel experience to an outstanding hotel experience. Izzy was well ahead of his time when it came to customer service excellence.

The first Four Seasons hotel was built in Toronto, Ontario Canada in the early 60's. It was a rather modest hotel by current standards but it was the beginning of a hotel empire founded on the golden rule ... "treat others as you would like to be treated." This rule was backed by an unrelenting commitment to providing an outstanding customer experience.

Exceeding customer expectations requires an acute ability to identify gaps in the first place and then bridge them with innovative product/ service solutions. And there was no one better at this skill than Izzy Sharp.

Izzy was known to have spent much of his time talking to customer's to uncover their desired reality outcomes and then evaluate them against current reality standards. Once those two reference points were known he went to work building bridges to span those gaps and deliver his customers to a superior hotel experience.

In fact, he was credited with the following service 'extras' that have since become 'standards' in the hotel industry.

- Shampoo bottles in all bathrooms (in the early days)
- Bathrobes and slippers in all rooms
- Telephones in the bathroom
- Workout facilities in all hotels
- Television sets in front of the treadmills and workout equipment

It is well documented that Izzy would often just show up unannounced to any one of his hotels and tour it through the eyes of a customer. He would stroll through the facility and recommend physical changes to the appearance of the front entrance, lobby and hotel rooms. He would listen to verbal exchanges and recommend protocol changes in how customers were greeted and moved through the check in experience. He would request services and recommend operational changes to how they were delivered. Izzy's discerning ears and eyes were constantly alert for ways to enhance the customer experience and he turned that commitment into a multi billion-dollar empire.

Izzy was well known for building the bridges necessary to deliver an outstanding customer experience but his true genius was in his ability to identify the gaps in the first place.

**The Result:**

Book a few nights at any Four Seasons Hotel or Resort and experience the results of Izzy's efforts for yourself.

# PART II

# THE PRESENTATION PHASE

In this part of the book you will learn how to
deliver *client-centric* presentations that
*separate* you from the competition
and *inspire* action.

# INTRODUCTION TO PRESENTATION

The second phase of the Gap Analysis Sales Model © is the PRESENTATION Phase.

> ➤ Have you ever delivered what you thought was a perfect presentation and yet failed to get the business? Or,
> ➤ Have you ever lost business to a competitor who offered a lower price or a reduced commission fee? Or,
> ➤ Have you ever had a client respond to your presentation with "leave it with me and I'll get back to you" and he didn't?

If you answered "yes" to either of these questions then you've suffered the consequence of a failed presentation.

If the ASSESSMENT phase defines the product/ service gap, then the PRESENTATION phase represents the bridge that spans the gap. Remember, everything you do and say during a sales presentation either accelerates or decelerates your forward momentum.

---

### PRESENTATION TIP:

Remember, everything you do and
say during a sales presentation
either accelerates or decelerates
your forward momentum.

---

The purpose of this part of the book is to show you how to accelerate your forward momentum by giving you the *insights, skills, and resources to deliver client-centric presentations that separate you from the competition and inspire action.*

A mentor of mine Jim Rohn once told me, "To be successful in life, simply do three things well: 1. Have something good to say, 2. Say it well and 3. Say it often." A successful presentation delivers on all three fronts: "having something good to say" refers to content, and "saying it well" refers to structure and delivery. When you are competent in these two areas you get invited to "say it often."

## Structure

Let's start off by addressing the importance of structure (saying it well). Structure is the first element of an effective presentation. It refers to the framework that sequences the flow of your information. Everything you do and say must be sequenced in a way that incrementally moves the client forward toward the desired outcome he or she wants to experience. Unskilled sales professionals often fail to organize their thoughts in a directional manner and subsequently deliver fractured presentations that confuse more than inspire.

In chapter four, you'll learn the most powerful way to structure your sales presentations. This structuring approach applies a whole-brain reasoning technique that appeals to both the logical (left side) and creative (right side) of the brain.

It is the same presentation strategy used by defense attorneys and prosecuting attorneys in a court of law. Now granted, you don't try cases for a living; yet every time you step in front of a client, you are, in essence, presenting **your** case to a jury of **your** peers and the acceptance or rejection of **your** proposal—rests in **their** hands.

## Content

The second element of an effective presentation is content (what you say). Have you ever noticed that you can say one thing to one client and he or she will feel utterly compelled to take action, while the same content delivered to another client will leave him or her completely uninspired? *Words*, *phrases*, *images*, and *evidence* that accelerate one person's buying decision may equally decelerate another's. It all comes down to each person's respective fears and desires.

Fears and desires are the two key motivators in life. As we discussed in the ASSESSMENT phase, knowing your client's psychometric profile will provide you with insights into both of these key motivators, as well as the types of evidence required to support a favorable decision.

Insights into tailoring your presentation content to align with your client's unique decision-making needs are addressed in chapter five.

## Delivery

The final element of an effective presentation is delivery. After all, you can have the finest content available, formatted within the ideal structure, and yet lose clients because you were unable to *capture their attention*, *hold their interest*, or *inspire them to take action*.

We've all had the experience of sitting through a presentation that elicited a feeling of boredom, anxiety or frustration. The reason this occurred was because the speaker's content and/ or delivery style did not align with our decision-making needs. The same holds true for the clients you engage. A presentation that is paced slower than your client's preferred processing speed will result in feelings of *frustration*. A presentation that is paced quicker than your client's preferred processing speed will result in a state of *anxiety*. Neither of these emotional states will support a favorable buying decision, even if your product/ service offering is ideally suited.

In fact, my experience confirms that the biggest mistake unskilled sales professionals make is that they design and deliver presentations to inspire themselves, **NOT THE CLIENT!**

---

### PRESENTATION TIP:

**The biggest mistake sales professionals
make is that they design and
deliver sales presentations to inspire
themselves, NOT THE CLIENT!**

---

Think about it: they say what **they** think is important, they provide evidence in a sequence that convinces **their** logical mind, they speak at a pace, tone, and volume that **they** themselves find pleasing. They are in essence selling to **themselves**, not the client, and unless the client has similar processing and decision-making needs, their presentation will fail miserably.

In chapter six you'll be introduced to a series of vocal and visual expression techniques that will add impact to your presentation and enhance long-term retention. You'll learn a number of audience involvement strategies to ensure that your sales presentation achieves the greatest impact.

In summary, the biggest mistake sales professionals make during the PRESENTATION phase of selling are:

- They fail to demonstrate a viable solution to the client problem.
- They fail to align with the client's unique decision-making needs.
- They fail to overcome the client's fear of taking action.

The Acceleration Strategies that follow will bridge these competency gaps by providing you with the tools to master the core skill of PRESENTATION.

~Chapter Four~
# Crafting Your Message

*Accelerate your selling success by convincing logically and inspiring emotionally.*

*"Tell them what you are going to tell them, tell them, and then tell them what you told them."*
– Teaching Credo

> *"Before I refuse to take your questions,*
> *I have an opening statement."*
> – Ronald Reagan

# LADIES AND GENTLEMEN OF THE JURY

## The GAP

When delivering a sales presentation, some sales professionals—forgive the expression—"show up and throw up." They just start talking, saying anything and everything that comes to mind hoping that the client can sift through the content to find the bits they need to support a buying decision. In the process, they leave the client feeling dazed, confused, and completely uninspired.

## The BRIDGE

As I mentioned before, defense attorneys rely on a powerful information sequencing strategy to convince their jury to return with a not guilty verdict. This sequencing strategy is founded in a three-part structural template. Here are the three elements of a strategically formatted presentation:

## Part 1: The Opening

Your sales presentation should begin with an eight- to eighteen-word statement that announces the purpose of your presentation. Known as the Statement of Intent (SOI), this opening statement might sound like:

> "We believe we can get this property fully leased in the time frame specified. Let me show you how." Or,
> "Here's how our company can save you over three hundred thousand a year in operating expenses." Or,

"I've put together an investment plan to achieve your financial goals; let me take you through my proposal."

Now you'll notice, in each case, that the SOI announces the client's *desired* reality objective. Just as in a court of law a defense attorney begins with an opening statement that points toward her client's acquittal, so too should you begin your presentation by directing your client toward his/ her desired reality outcome.

The SOI serves three purposes:

1. *To establish intent:* This allows the listener to focus on what you are saying rather than trying to figure out what you are going to cover.
2. *To confirm direction:* This provides a clear destination point that your clients will recognize when you take them there.
3. *To establish a standard:* This provides a reference point from which to evaluate the effectiveness of your presentation.

You may have noticed that each chapter of this book begins with an eight- to eighteen-word SOI. This one was to show you how to *"accelerate your selling success by convincing logically and inspiring emotionally"* — ten words that identify purpose, confirm direction and establish a reference point.

Everything that follows your SOI should consist of the information or strategy that will take the client to where he or she wants to get to. If it doesn't, then it simply doesn't belong in your presentation.

## Part 2: The Main Body
When designing your written or verbal presentation, consider segmenting the main body of your presentation into three parts. Why

three-parts and not two or four-parts? Because **three** reasons, **three** action steps, or **three** benefits will ideally satisfy your client's logical decision-making needs. A two-part plan is too shaky to support a big decision and a four (or more)-part plan can be too overwhelming and confusing to consider.

"Three" is the magic number. Just as a bridge requires three pillars to support its center span, so too does it take three pillars to support the client's logical decision-making needs.

---

## PRESENTATION TIP:

**"Three" is the magic number.
Just as a bridge requires three
pillars to support its center span,
so too does it take three pillars
to support the client's logical
decision-making needs.**

---

Think about it: a homeowner typically gets three estimates before adding a new deck or swimming pool. A car shopper typically tries out three different styles of automobiles before settling on one. The homebuyer, before writing an offer on one property, typically requires two others as comparables to help justify the offer price.

Retailers have long known about the "magic of three." Most products or services are made available to the consuming public in three choices. Gas comes in three different grades (regular, premium, and supreme). Automobiles come in three different models (base, mid, and high end). Airfares come disguised in three different classes (coach, business class, and first class). Even most sporting events have three different seat pricing tiers (floor level, mezzanine, and nosebleed). Why, because consumers want to have two secondary reference points from which to support one primary purchase decision.

This book follows this same principle. It is segmented into three parts:

Part 1: The ASSESSMENT Phase

Part 2: The PRESENTATION Phase

Part 3: The NEGOTIATION Phase

Each of these parts is broken down into three sub-parts (chapters) and then each of these subparts is flushed out into sub-sub-parts (Acceleration Strategies). Why? Because the logical mind finds it easier to remember information sequenced in this delivery format!

Regardless of what product/ service presentation you deliver, you should sequence it using this format. A real estate sales agent might structure a listing presentation using the following three-part plan:

Part 1: Market Overview

Part 2: Marketing Strategy

Part 3: Sales Team (and roles)

This particular three-part plan incorporates everything a homeowner requires to support a listing decision, plus it puts it into a logical sequence. Properly delivered, this sequence *"convinces logically and inspires emotionally."*

## Part 3: The Conclusion

An effective conclusion consists of two elements: A *summary statement* and a *call to action*. The *summary statement* is simply a reaffirmation of your opening Statement of Intention followed by a quick recap of your three-part plan.

The same listing real estate agent might summarize his presentation by saying, "John, I've provided an overview of what's driving today's market. I've put together a pricing strategy and marketing campaign that capitalizes on these conditions and finally

I've introduced you to my team who will handle every detail of this transaction for you." That's your *summary statement*! The words that follow are known as the *call to action* and are vital if you are to move the process forward.

The *call to action* does not always have to involve the signing of an agreement. In some cases a *call to action* might be to set up a subsequent meeting or to research additional information. The main thing is that you continue to move the process forward, by a large leap or a small step, depending on your perception of the client's readiness.

If it's not appropriate to ask for the business, then ask the client to take a logical next step:

"Why don't we get together at the end of this week to give you some time to discuss this with your partner?" Or,

"I can have that additional information for you by tomorrow. Why don't we get together at 4:00 p.m. to iron out the details?" Or,

"What would you like the next steps to be?"

A sales presentation without a *call to action* is not a sales presentation at all; it is an information dump that will fall short of its objective to inspire action.

---

### PRESENTATION TIP:

A sales presentation without a
*call to action* is not a sales presentation
at all; it is an information dump
that will fall short of its objective
to inspire action.

---

It's like a golf putt that comes up short of the hole. It never had a chance. Putt past the hole! Be willing to go the distance by asking for the business or by requesting the next logical step be taken. After all, if you don't ask you won't get.

It's also important to consider that your *call to action* be tailored to your client's **DISC**-based buyer profile. You'll learn exactly how to do this in chapter five.

A solid presentation structure may seem rigid initially, but your perseverance will be rewarded. Although you might find it to be uncomfortable to apply at first, there are nine tangible benefits to delivering a well formatted and highly structured sales presentation. They are:

1. **You don't miss anything:** Everything gets covered because everything is sequenced in a logical order and serves a specific purpose.

2. **It keeps you on track:** It's hard to get off track when you are following a straight line. If you do get pulled off track, it is easy to jump back on and carry on where you left off.

3. **It places you firmly in control:** An effective structure allows you to instantly shorten or lengthen a presentation as required by the client.

4. **It is replicable:** A structure provides a template that can be used over and over again. The only thing you change in a structured presentation is the content and the style of your delivery.

5. **It is adaptable to changing needs:** If, during your sales presentation, it becomes evident that you need to spend more time on one part of your presentation than others, you can adjust accordingly.

6. **It is easy to follow:** Strong structure is like using GPS. It's easy to reflect on where you have been, identify where you are, and confirm where you are heading.

7. **It generates momentum:** Each part of the three-part plan moves the client incrementally forward, across the bridge, toward his/ her desired end objective.

8. **It is more professional:** If two people deliver the identical content, the person who utilizes the best structure will always be deemed more professional.

9. **And finally, because of benefits 1 through 8, IT WORKS:** It produces tangible results! I've had entire offices, after adapting to the GAP analysis presentation strategy; confirm that they went from a 40% presentation success rate to 90% literally overnight.

An effective structure affords you a considerable edge by separating yourself from the competition and making it easier for your clients to say, *"yes"* to your product/ service offering.

---

**PRESENTATION ACTION PLAN**

---

**⟳━INSIGHTS:**

Know that the purpose of your presentation is to demonstrate how your product/ service offering is a bridge that will take your clients from where they are *(current reality)* to where they want to be *(desired reality)*.

**⟳━SKILLS:**

Apply a presentation strategy that consists of:

- An eight- to eighteen-word SOI that announces the purpose of your presentation.

- A three-part structure to house your presentation content.

- A *summary statement* and a *call to action* at the conclusion of your presentation.

> *"Begin at the beginning and go on till*
> *you come to the end: Then stop!"*
> – The King (Alice in Wonderland)

# IT'S AS EASY AS 1, 2, 3

## The GAP

Most sales professionals fail to organize their sales message in a way that *"convinces logically and inspires emotionally."* As a result, the uninspired client fails to take action on the product/ service offering.

## The BRIDGE

There are eight formatting options that can be used to sequence your content into a three-part plan. The format you choose should be aligned with the type of information being conveyed. Here are the various ways you can structure your three-part plan and sub-plans:

## 1. The "Benefit Analysis"

This approach could be used to deliver a sales presentation that demonstrates the multiple benefits of your product/ service offering. A recreational vehicle sales consultant might use this approach to communicate the benefits of one specific line of motor home over others. For instance:

> SOI: There are several reasons why I recommend this manufacturer over the other lines we have in stock. Here is the top three.
>> Part 1: Benefit #1—Affordability
>> Part 2: Benefit #2—Functionality
>> Part 3. Benefit #3—Reliability

## 2. The "Comparative Analysis"

This formatting option can be used to deliver a sales presentation that compares the features and benefits of one product/ service offering over other similar offerings. A real estate project marketer might use this approach to communicate the lifestyle benefits of one development project over other similar projects. For example:

> SOI: Here's a comparison of how this lifestyle community stacks up against the two others in the city.
> Part 1: Condominium Project #1
> Part 2: Condominium Project #2
> Part 3: Condominium Project #3

The difference between the benefit analysis and the comparative analysis is that the benefit analysis allows you to focus on one specific product/ service offering while the comparative analysis allows you to compare multiple offerings.

## 3. The "Chronologic Analysis"

Use this approach to deliver a presentation that demonstrates growth over a specific period of time. An investment broker might use this approach to convey an investment yield over a specified period of time. For example:

> SOI: This investment has experienced steady growth over the past ten years and continues to have upside potential. Let me show you why I'm recommending it to my core clients.
> Part 1. Historical performance
> Part 2. Current value
> Part 3. Projected growth *

* Note: Be mindful when making future growth projections. Ensure that you disclose your sources and confirm that you're not making a representation of real growth.

## 4. The "Concentric Analysis"

This approach could be used to communicate a broadening or narrowing perspective of a specific product line, service offering or region. A commercial real estate agent might use this approach to narrow the parameters of an office lease search. For example:

> SOI: Let me give you an overall perspective of the local real estate market.
> Part 1. Greater Vancouver
> Part 2. Downtown Vancouver
> Part 3. Robson Street

This formatting strategy is ideal for information-based presentations in which the primary objective is to provide a macro perspective to support a micro decision.

## 5. The "Topical Analysis"

Use this approach to deliver a presentation on a subject that can be segmented by topic. A financial planner might use this approach to deliver a presentation on a wealth creation strategy for a client. For example:

> SOI: There are a number of wealth building strategies available. Let me show you three that we recommend for our clients:
> Part 1. Real Estate
> Part 2. Stock Market
> Part 3. Bond Market

## 6. The "Transitional Analysis"

This approach could be used to introduce a staggered implementation schedule. A telecommunication consultant might use this approach to communicate a strategy for system integration. For example:

SOI: Here's how I recommend we integrate our telecommunication system into your existing network:
    Part 1. Phase 1 Integration Strategy
    Part 2. Phase 2 Integration Strategy
    Part 3. Phase 3 Integration Strategy

## 7. The "Categorical Analysis"

Use this approach to deliver a presentation on a subject that can be segmented categorically. A residential real estate agent might use this format to introduce the benefits of different types of home ownership. For example:

SOI: To facilitate your buying decision, I've identified some of the major differences between the three home ownership options:
    Part 1. Detached Home
    Part 2. Townhouse
    Part 3. Condominium

## 8. The "Hierarchical Analysis"

This approach can be used to deliver a presentation on a topic that can be segmented into different levels of price or performance. An auto salesperson might use this format to define the differences between models. For example:

SOI: Here are the various options available to you with this particular vehicle:
    Part 1. Base Model Options
    Part 2. Sport Model Options
    Part 3. Luxury Model Options

As I stated earlier, this book follows a very linear three-part plan with each part sequenced using one of these specific formatting strategies. The main part of the book is structured using a *transitional* three-part plan:

Part 1. The ASSESSMENT Phase
Part 2. The PRESENTATION Phase
Part 3. The NEGOTIATION Phase

This *transitional* three-part plan is further divided into individual three-part sub-plans:

PART 1: The ASSESSMENT Phase is segmented *topically* under three chapter headings:
Chapter 1: Sales Profiles
Chapter 2: Buyer Profiles
Chapter 3: Gap Analysis

PART 2: The PRESENTATION Phase is segmented *topically* under three chapter headings:
Chapter 4: Crafting Your Message
Chapter 5: Tailoring Your Content
Chapter 6: Strengthening Your Delivery

PART 3: The NEGOTIATION Phase is also segmented *topically* under three chapter headings:
Chapter 7: Power Sources
Chapter 8: Negotiating Stress
Chapter 9: Tactics/Counter Tactics

Now, if you were to dig down deeper you'd find that each one of these three-part sub-plans were further divided into two or three-part sub-sub-plans. Why? Because it is the easiest format and structure for you to follow, and the more you follow the more you'll remember, the more you remember the more you'll transfer to your workplace.

Whichever formatting option you decide to use in your three-part plan or sub plan, be sure to check in with your client at the transition points of your presentation. A skilled presenter will ensure that the client is in agreement with the information being presented; after all if your client does not agree with what you're saying, his/ her forward momentum stops at that point. Sample agreement phrases include: "Are we on the same page?" "Does this make sense to you?" "Does this sound reasonable?" and "Are we aligned in our thinking?"

If the client responds with "yes," that's a good thing! It means your client is standing beside you on your bridge. In this case the next step is to take her further down the bridge, check again, and finally take her to the other side.

Now, if the client responds with "no" at any point of your presentation, that's also a good thing! It tells you that she is lagging behind and that to continue your sales presentation would be fruitless. So rather than carrying on, take a step back, uncover the lingering fears or doubts that have halted her forward momentum, address them, and then carry on together.

---

### PRESENTATION ACTION PLAN

---

**○━━INSIGHTS:**

Know that a presentation that *convinces logically* and *inspires emotionally* is also easy to say, "Yes" to.

**○━━SKILLS:**

Apply a highly structured message sequencing strategy when designing and delivering a presentation for your prospective client.

**○━━RESOURCES:**

Refer to the eight formatting strategies identified in this Acceleration Strategy and select the one best suited to convey your information.

~Chapter Five~

# Aligning Your Content

*Accelerate your selling success by aligning your sales message with your client's decision-making needs.*

*"In the right key one can say anything, in the wrong key nothing. The only delicate part is the establishment of the key."*
— George Bernard Shaw

> *"Most sales people deliver sales presentations that are designed and delivered to inspire themselves, not the client."*
> – Gerald G. Clerx

# RIGHT DOOR – WRONG KEY!

### The GAP

Most sales professionals neglect to account for the unique decision-making needs of their clients and as a result fail to inspire a favorable buying decision.

### The BRIDGE

It simply isn't enough to have the right product/ service solution to bridge your client's gap. You must also be able to communicate the value of your offering in a way that aligns with his/ her unique decision-making needs.

A client's **DISC** profile is the *key* that influences both what the client needs to hear or see (content) and how he or she needs to hear it (structure and delivery). Before we move on let's make some distinctions here; content refers to anything the client hears or sees, including words, phrases, images, and evidence.

### Verbal Content

From a **DISC** perspective there are two profile groups who prefer content that is collaborative. The words "we," "let's", and "together" are examples of collaborative words. The phrase "Here is what <u>we</u> should consider before taking <u>our</u> next steps together," speaks to the need for collaboration of effort.

The other two profile groups prefer words that are outcome-focused and non-collaborative such as "I" and "you." The statement

"Here is how I intend to achieve the results you are after" speaks to the need for delineation of responsibility.

As a point of fact, non-collaborative clients can become quite frustrated by collaborative speaking salespeople. They may tolerate it for a while but its continued use will likely elicit a rather firmly directed corrective statement such as, "Look **WE** aren't doing anything—**YOU** are! That's why I am paying **YOU**!

Another form of content is evidence. Evidence is used to alleviate fears and each profile group responds favorably to the evidence that addresses their own respective fear. For instance, the greatest fear of the high D is "fear of failure," therefore a presentation to a member of this profile group ought to include evidence that demonstrates how your product/ service will help him or her to achieve a *successful outcome*.

---

**PRESENTATION TIP:**

**A client's DISC profile will tell you
a great deal about the type of
evidence (and how much of it) to
include in your sales presentation.**

---

High I's require very little evidence to support a decision because much of their decision to move forward will come down to the strength of your relationship.

High S's fear "loss of stability"; therefore, your presentation ought to be ripe with evidence confirming your ability to bring stability to their environment.

The greatest fear of high C's is "making a mistake." In this case, your presentation ought to be ripe with all forms of evidence pointing to the fact that they are making the right decision, as well as some warranties and guarantees thrown in for good measure.

A client's **DISC** profile also influences what they want to see. One profile group responds favorably to dramatic images accompanied by bold statements, while another prefers conservative images supported by factual analysis.

Your personal appearance also plays a role in how clients respond to you. How you appear and act naturally appeals to only one of the four buying styles; has moderate appeal to two others and negatively impacts the remaining group. Now think about this statistic for a moment. It's worth considering! You frustrate the heck out of approximately 25 percent of the clients you stand in front of, just by being who you are.

---

### PRESENTATION TIP:

**You frustrate the heck out of approximately 25 percent of the clients you stand in front of, just by being who you are.**

---

Tailoring the *verbal* and *visual* content of your presentation to align with the **DISC** profile of your client is more important than you might realize. Delivering a high **I** style sales presentation to a high **C** client is like speaking Italian to a person who only understands German.

Likewise, delivering a high **D** presentation to a high **S** client is the equivalent of speaking Bulgarian to a Canadian. You might get a courteous nod periodically, but the client is simply buying time until he or she finds an appropriate opportunity to disengage.

A client's **DISC** profile should also be considered in the way you open your presentation (SOI), the way you conclude it (*summary statement* and *call to action*), and the pace in which you deliver everything in between.

These **DISC**-based presentation alignment techniques are the subject of the following four Acceleration Strategies.

---

### PRESENTATION ACTION PLAN

---

○──INSIGHTS:

Know that "In the right key one can say anything and in the wrong key nothing" and that everything you do and say during your presentation needs to be in alignment with your client's decision-making "keys."

○──SKILLS:

Apply a DISC-based tailoring strategy to ensure that your sales presentation aligns with the *content, structure,* and *delivery* needs of your client.

# LET ME GET RIGHT TO THE POINT

### The GAP

Most sales professionals fail to communicate their product/ service offering in a way that aligns with the unique *content* and *delivery* needs of the high **D** client.

### The BRIDGE

There are five behavioral *keys* you need to consider when presenting your product/ service solution to members of this profile group:

> ➢ They are *task focused.*
> ➢ They are *behaviorally active.*
> ➢ They fear failure.
> ➢ They desire quick results, and
> ➢ They are influenced by your ability to *get the job done.*

You may want to read these critical decision-making keys again; after all, when presenting to a high **D** client the success of your presentation is tied to your ability to align with each one of them.

High **D** clients respond to sales presentations differently than their **DISC** counterparts. Here are ten ways to accelerate your success when presenting to a **D** client:

### 1. Align your *Statement of Intention* (SOI)

Begin your presentation with an SOI that promises a successful outcome achieved in a timely fashion. Remember, every sales presentation represents a bridge that spans your client's product/

service gap. In the case of the high **D** client, he wants your bridge to support a quick and successful outcome. "Let me show you how our company can save your company $300,000 in annual operating costs," or "Here's how my team will get your building leased up in the time frame specified," or "Here's how I can double your investment in the next 6 months!" These opening statements all speak to the needs of the high **D** client.

## 2. Demonstrate the quality of *professional confidence*

Carry yourself and communicate your product/ service offering with confidence and certainty. The client wants to see in you the qualities they admire most about themselves. Remember, **D**'s are quick to judge so make sure your first impression is a professional one. If it isn't, you'll be fighting through the balance of your presentation, if he allows you to continue at all.

## 3. Communicate in a style that is *direct and to the point*

High **D**'s do not want you to mince words, skirt issues, or dress things up for them. They expect you to tell it like it is, even if the news isn't great. But they also expect you to take responsibility for your actions and to be ready to execute at a moment's notice.

If you don't know the answer to a question asked of you, say so and affirm your commitment to find out. When responding to questions, replace weak words and phrases with direct and affirmative language. For Example:

|  | **Weak** |  | **Affirmative** |
|---|---|---|---|
| Replace | *I'll try to...* | with | *I will...* |
| Replace | *I'll see what I can do.* | with | *I'll take care of it!* |
| Replace | *Maybe (or Perhaps!)* | with | *Yes (or Certainly!)* |
| Replace | *I'm not sure.* | with | *I'll find out!* |
| Replace | *That's not my problem!* | with | *I'll take care of it!* |

## 4. Use words that are *actively* paced and *outcome* focused

When presenting your product/ service offering to a high **D**, your language should include words like *results, achieve, realize, driven, successful track record, accomplish*, and *priority*. Phrases that also align with this profile group include:

> *Here's the bottom line.*
> *Let me get right to the point for you.*
> *I'll cut to the chase.*
> *Here's what we know.*
> *I'll handle it.* And of course,
> *I'm on it!*

High **D**'s respond favorably to this type of language because it aligns with both their task focused nature and active behavioral pace.

## 5. Use powerful images that *convey results*

Images integrated into a high **D** presentation ought to capture the client's desired end objective. Inspect any car ad targeting to this group and you'll notice the car is black, silver, or navy; it's in motion and it's accompanied by a bold caption promising to deliver what the high **D** seeks. Here are some examples of **D**-targeted campaign slogans:

> "Follow no one!"
> "When you are in the lead, no one spoils your view."
> "Revered, Admired, Praised. But still unchallenged."
> "We think about unfair advantages."
> "Built for the left side of the brain and the right foot."

The last one is one of my favorites because it fits right into the high **D** quadrant defined by logic (left side of the brain) and speed (right foot).

## 6. Follow a *linear* structure

When presenting to a high **D**, do not deviate from your linear structure unless asked to do so. Stay on a direct pathway and if you do inadvertently stray off track respond immediately to set things right with "Let me get back on track!" Then do it!

## 7. Support their desire for *quick results*

Your presentation should demonstrate how you will achieve a quick and successful outcome. The phrase "Time is money" is the rallying cry of the high **D** profile group. They don't like to be put on hold, stand in line, get stuck in traffic or worse yet be presented to by someone who is taking too long to get to the point. Express check-in and checkout counters at hotels, airports, and car rental agencies were all established in response to this psychometric pet peeve. American Express created the "Front of the Line" campaign to support this inherent need to jump the queue.

## 8. Alleviate their *fear of failure*

Quite simply stated, high **D**'s don't like to fail. A failed outcome plays against their ego identity. Your presentation should therefore reinforce the fact that you, your team, and/ or your company are all poised to help your client achieve a successful outcome. By the way, of the four profile groups, high **D**'s are most inclined to award you the business if you are the leader in your respective industry or market. They like to associate with those who they perceive as "best in class."

## 9. Convince with *factual* evidence:

High **D** clients are predominantly logic based and are therefore influenced by factual evidence, especially when delivered in an executive summary format. Pie charts and bar graphs that provide a summarized overview strongly align with their decision-making needs. Let them know you've done the research to justify your recommendations, but don't mire them in your findings during your presentation.

## 10. Align your *call to action*:

Gain commitment with a *call to action* statement that shows a willingness to get started right away while allowing them to call the play. A service provider might align their call to action with: "My team is poised and ready to get started on this project—we just need you to give us the green light." A sales person might align with: "I can have this ready for you to pick up tomorrow at 10 AM sharp. I just need your authorization."

Make a mental note to never force a high D's hand or apply a high-pressure closing technique, as they are not fond of others attempting to direct their actions.

---

### PRESENTATION TIP:

**High D's are silently evaluating you on your ability to get the job done so make sure that you act like a competent and capable professional.**

---

Understand that high D's are silently evaluating you on your ability to get the job done so make sure that you look and act like a competent and capable professional.

When you follow these presentation tips to members of this profile group, you align with their decision-making needs and by doing so you accelerate a successful outcome.

## PRESENTATION ACTION PLAN

**O——INSIGHTS:**

Know that high **D**'s desire *quick results,* fear *failure,* and are influenced by your ability to *get the job done.*

**O——SKILLS:**

Apply a presentation strategy that:

- Aligns with the high **D**'s "no frills" *content* needs.

- Aligns with the high **D**'s highly directional *structure* needs.

- Aligns with the high **D**'s fast paced *delivery* needs.

> *"Engage me, acknowledge me and connect with me."*
> – High I Buying Motto

# You Look Marvelous!

**The GAP**

Most sales professionals fail to communicate their product/ service offering in a way that aligns with the unique *content* and *delivery* needs of the high **I** client.

**The BRIDGE**

Now granted, not all high **I**'s "look marvelous," as the title above suggests, but it is in their nature to appreciate sincere compliments directed their way. Here are five behavioral *keys* you must consider when presenting your product/ service solution to high **I** clients:

- ➤ They are *relationship focused.*
- ➤ They are *behaviorally active.*
- ➤ They fear *loss of influence.*
- ➤ They desire *recognition* and *acknowledgement.*
- ➤ They are largely influenced by *the personal connection they feel toward you.*

High **I** clients respond to sales presentations differently than their **DISC** counterparts. Here are ten ways to accelerate your success with members of this profile group:

## 1. Align your *Statement of Intention* (SOI)

Begin your presentation with an SOI that promises an exclusive offering or an innovative solution. An example of this might be:

"John, you are going to love what I have to show you", or "Mary I've located the ideal home for you!"

## 2. Demonstrate the qualities of *friendliness* and *likeability*

High I's want to see in you what they admire most about themselves. They are gregarious and outgoing by nature and they don't mind engaging in a bit of relationship-building discourse. It is through this mutual exchange that commonalities are established and relationships forged. There is no bigger turnoff for a high I than to meet someone who is not interesting, or worse yet, not interested.

## 3. Communicate in a style that is *interactive* and *engaging*

Perhaps the biggest need for high I clients is to feel engaged. They like to be given the opportunity to speak their mind, so give it to them. It's also wise to budget plenty of time for your presentation, as they're not afraid to offer up an opinion to someone ready and willing to listen. Keep in mind that I's have a limited attention span and will therefore need to be engaged far more frequently than the other profile groups. For the most part, high I's love to laugh, so keep it light.

## 4. Use language that is *actively* paced and *socially* directed

High I's appreciate a livelier and more colorful vocabulary than the other profile groups. In advertising campaigns directed toward them you'll notice a strong reliance on words like *enthusiastic, entertaining, lively, optimistic, wholeheartedly, inspiring,* and *passionate.* These are descriptors that high I's connect with, so sprinkle them liberally throughout your presentation. Depending on your product/ service offering they'll also respond favorably to phrases such as:

> *That's a great idea!*
> *You'll love what I have to show you!*
> *This is brilliant!*

## 5. Use colorful images that *convey excitement*

Since high I's are highly visual, your presentation content should align accordingly. Bright colors, striking images and bold text are heavily employed in advertising campaigns directed toward this profile group. Here are some real life examples of captions found on some recent auto advertisements:

"Go topless" (referencing a convertible).

"Loves to run!"

"0–60 in a heart-pounding 4.3 seconds!"

"It'll cause your symptoms to accelerate!"

"If you're going to be late you might as well be fashionably late!"

## 6. Follow a *nonlinear* structure

When presenting to a high I it's okay to take an indirect route. Make sure you're heading in the right general direction; however, don't be afraid to take the occasional detour to investigate a topic of mutual interest.

While it's not necessary to get right down to business, it is important to keep things moving, even if it's a lateral move. You can take the high I client off track periodically and still have a productive meeting. Ask questions about something you know she has an interest in; however, be prepared to segue way back onto topic if she begins to stray a little too far off track.

## 7. Support their desire for *acknowledgment* and *recognition*

Your presentation should sincerely acknowledge the high I's accomplishments as they relate to your product/ service offering. High I's are ego based and appreciate being recognized for their accomplishments.

I once witnessed a commercial real estate agent begin her office leasing presentation to a high I client with the following SOI: "We think you have the sexiest building in town, let me show you how we intend to get it fully leased up with equally attractive tenants." I thought it was a bit of a stretch for her to refer to the subject building as *"sexy,"* but the client didn't. He was sold the moment she said it. She won the business handily over more experienced competitors, who had apparently failed to recognize and acknowledge the building's obvious physical attributes.

### 8. Alleviate their fear of *loss of influence*

The high I's ego identity is tied to his/ her ability to influence others, and when you seek out your client's opinion, you align with that psychological need.

### 9. Convince with *stories* and *case studies*

High I's are not known for their pragmatic approach or their attention to detail. Rather than facts or figures, they respond far better to stories and testimonials, especially if they're familiar with the project or person referenced.

### 10. Align your *call to action*

Gain commitment with a *call to action* statement that is both collaborative and enthusiastic. An example might be, "We're excited about working with you and eager to get started! Shall we get the ball rolling?" Note that this *call to action* sounds nothing like the one recommended to the high D client.

---

**PRESENTATION TIP:**

**High I's are silently evaluating you
on your likeability factor.**

---

Keep in mind that high I's are silently evaluating you on your likeability factor. Sure it's important that you have a suitable product choice or service capability, but for them, you must be someone they'll enjoy doing business with. "Do I like this person?" is a question often posed by their inner dialogue.

When you follow these presentation tips to members of this profile group, you align with their decision-making needs and by doing so you accelerate a favorable buying decision.

---

### PRESENTATION ACTION PLAN

---

**O——INSIGHTS:**

**Know** that high I's desire *acknowledgement* and *recognition*, fear *loss of influence*, and are quietly evaluating you on your *likeability factor*.

**O——SKILLS:**

**Apply** a presentation strategy that:

- Aligns with the high I's more stimulating *content* needs.

- Aligns with the high I's flexible *structure* needs.

- Aligns with the high I's interactive and engaging *delivery* needs.

> *"I don't care how much you know*
> *until I know how much you care."*
> – High S Buying Motto

# TRUST ME!

## The GAP

Most sales professionals fail to communicate their product/ service offering in a way that aligns with the unique *content* and *delivery* needs of the high S client.

## The BRIDGE

High S's are strongly influenced by your level of trustworthiness. Granted, trust is an important consideration in any relationship; however, with the high S it's extremely important.

There are five behavioral *keys* you need to consider when presenting your product/ service solution to high S clients:

> They are *socially focused.*
> They are *behaviorally passive.*
> They fear *loss of stability* (change).
> They desire *safety* and *security.*
> They are influenced by *those they trust.*

High S clients respond to sales presentations differently than their **DISC** counterparts. Here are ten ways to accelerate your success with members of this profile group:

### 1. Align your *Statement of Intention* (SOI)

Begin your presentation with an SOI that confirms an understanding of the client's needs and concerns. For instance: "Mary, this proposal considers the objectives you've identified and addresses the concerns you raised earlier." This conversational approach is an ideal way to set the tone of your presentation with high S's.

## 2. Demonstrate the qualities of *empathy* and *commitment*

High S's appreciate seeing in you the qualities they themselves emulate. So stop talking and start listening. Be attentive to the client and empathetic to his/ her feelings. Empathy represents the highest level of listening and it takes a quiet mind and a dedicated effort to get to this level.

## 3. Communicate in a style that is both *collaborative* and *respectful*

Remain calm and patient, at all times. High S's do not respond favorably to a confrontational approach. In fact, aggressive posturing will cause them to retreat into a position of quiet defiance. They may not vocalize their resentment as loudly as the previous two profile groups, but don't be fooled—their resolve is just as strong. And don't attempt to rush their decision either as they would rather decide on their own time schedule. Assure them that you're there as a "success partner"—not as a "salesperson."

## 4. Use language that is *passively* paced and *relationship* focused

High S profiles speak the language of collaboration. Words like *we, together,* and *let's* are appreciated by this profile group. They also respond favorably to words such as *family, empathize, secure, comfortable, collaborate,* and *cooperate,* so be sure to incorporate them into your presentation. The following phrases also appeal to the high S:

> *I understand.*
> *That seems fair.*
> *I can appreciate that.*
> *What can we do to resolve this?*
> *What else would support you in your decision?*

Notice that these non-defensive phrases are rooted in a spirit of cooperation and collaboration, which is the preferred language for the high S.

## 5. Use traditional images that *convey safety*

In advertising campaigns directed toward high S's, earth tones such as whites, greens, browns, and blues are strongly promoted. Flashy and powerful images don't work with this group so don't use them. Family, safety, and security are all strong emotional anchors for the high S, so build them into your presentation, if practical. Here are some real world examples of auto advertising campaigns targeting members of this profile group:

"Give them love, compassion, sheet metal and steel."

"Experience the tranquility of Avalon."

"For you, time with your best friend is important."

## 6. Follow a *nonlinear* structure

When presenting to the high S client, it's OK to take an occasional detour, especially to inquire about any underlying concerns he or she may have regarding your product, your proposal, or the company you represent.

## 7. Support their desire for *safety and security*

Your presentation should highlight the safety features of your product/ service offering and the associated benefits. Not only must the client feel safe with your offering she must also feel safe with you. Trust is a big piece of the high S puzzle so be trust "worthy."

## 8. Alleviate their fear of *loss of stability*

When selling to high S's, take it slow. This group does not like to be rushed and is not comfortable with change. High S's are risk intolerant and will shut down if they begin to feel overwhelmed. During your sales presentation, check in with them periodically. Ask if they have any questions or concerns after each main part of your presentation. If they do, answer them, and check in to make sure the answer satisfactorily addressed their concern before moving on.

## 9. Convince with *testimonial evidence*

High S's are influenced more by the opinion of others than they are by facts and figures. A third party testimonial carries far more decision-making weight, especially if he/ she is known. Facts and figures are too impersonal to convince this relationship-driven client. Being the "biggest company" or "top producer" means nothing to the high S unless it can be linked to safety and security.

## 10. Align your *call to action*

Gain commitment with a *call to action* statement that is both collaborative and low pressure. An example might be: "Mary, if you are comfortable with my team and our commitment to this project, I'd like to recommend we take the next step." Never try to close the high S with high-pressure techniques learned in years past. A presentation that is too rushed or high pressure for a high S will inevitably lead to feelings of anxiety that will result in one of the following classic "put off" responses:

> Why don't you leave it with me, or
> I just want to run this by my partner, or
> I'll call you when I'm ready to make a decision.

If you hear either of these response phrases, recognize it as the high S's way of telling you that she is feeling anxious or frustrated. Unless you back off, you won't hear from her again.

---

### PRESENTATION TIP:

High S's are silently evaluating you
on your level of trustworthiness,
so do what you say you're
going to do.

---

High S's are silently evaluating you on your level of trustworthiness, so do what you say you are going to do.

When you follow these presentation tips to members of the high S profile group, you align with their decision-making needs and by doing so you accelerate a favorable buying decision.

---

## PRESENTATION ACTION PLAN

---

**O—►INSIGHTS:**

**Know** that high S's desire a *safe* and *secure* outcome, they fear *change*, and they are quietly evaluating you on your level of *trustworthiness*.

**O—►SKILLS:**

**Apply** a presentation strategy that:

- Aligns with the high S's reassuring *content* needs.

- Aligns with the high S's moderate *structure* needs.

- Aligns with the high S's steady and deliberate *delivery* needs.

# HERE ARE THE FACTS

### The GAP

Most sales professionals fail to communicate their product/ service offering in a way that aligns with the unique *content* and *delivery* needs of the high **C** client.

### The BRIDGE

High **C**'s LOVE facts! Why? Because their greatest psychological fear is the fear of making a mistake! Evidence minimizes the likelihood of mistakes occurring, so they feel more at ease when you arm them with plenty of the right evidence to support their left-brain decision-making needs.

There are five behavioral characteristics you need to consider when presenting your product/ service solution to high **C** clients:

➢ They are *task oriented*.
➢ They are *behaviorally passive*.
➢ They fear *making mistakes*.
➢ They desire *accuracy of information*.
➢ They are influenced by *their perception of your subject matter expertise.*

High **C** clients respond to sales presentations differently than their **DISC** counterparts. Here are ten ways to accelerate your success with members of this profile group:

## 1. Align your *Statement of Intention* (SOI)

Begin your presentation with an accurate SOI that promises a specific outcome backed by evidence. An example of this might be: "Our Company can save you $328,000 in operating expenses per year. Let me show you how," or "Based on current market conditions, your property should net 2.8 million. Here are the comparables that justify this value."

## 2. Demonstrate the quality of *professional competence*

High C's place great value on competence and accuracy. Competence extends beyond what you say; it also includes what the client sees, so make sure to double-check your reports, documents, and PowerPoint presentations. Even minor spelling or grammatical errors will raise competency concerns from members of this profile group.

## 3. Communicate in a style that is both *logical* and *consistent*

High C's appreciate communication rooted in logic and reason, so be sure your presentation follows a logical sequence. Also ensure that you check for agreement each step of the way; after all, if a high C doesn't agree with one aspect of your presentation, he or she will certainly not comply with your *call to action.*

## 4. Use language that is *passively paced* and *outcome focused*

The following words appeal to the high C's pragmatic and systematic approach to making decisions: *analysis, accuracy, assurance, systematic, detailed, logical,* and *measurable.* The following phrases also appeal to members of this profile group:

> *The facts suggest...*
> *Based on the evidence, I recommend...*
> *Logically speaking...*
> *It follows that...*
> *Here is a comprehensive analysis of...*

## 5. Use conservative images that *convey reliability*

High C's are the most conservative of all four profile groups. Since conservative colors are brown, grey, and navy you'll notice these as dominant colors in advertising campaigns targeting this group. These are often combined with logic-based promotional slogans, such as:

"Tell yourself it's a rational decision."

"Where logic and reason meet."

"The obvious choice for today's intelligent consumer."

## 6. Follow a very *linear* structure

When presenting to the high C, it's imperative that you follow a linear route unless otherwise directed. I assure you this will be the longest client engagement process you'll ever endure as the merits of your product/ service recommendations are carefully weighed against other options. Don't be discouraged by the length of time it takes for a high C to render a decision; after all, a quick decision is usually one that dismisses your product/ service offering.

## 7. Support their *desire for accuracy*

Your presentation should be comprehensive and double-checked for accuracy. Make sure the information presented is current and obtained from reliable sources. A great deal of the high C's decision will hinge upon their perception of your professional credibility.

## 8. Alleviate their *fear of making a mistake*

The high C's greatest fear is of making a mistake. Alleviate this fear with a comprehensive overview of the product/ service offering backed by personal assurances and performance guarantees. Both approaches are effective at overcoming high C buying anxiety.

## 9. Convince with *statistical* evidence

Once again, high C's are influenced by logic and reason. Provide them with statistical evidence to support your recommendations.

*Facts, figures,* and *case studies* carry the most weight with this group because of their objective nature. *Testimonials* from credible sources can also be effective at swaying a decision in your favor.

## 10. Align your *call to action*

Gain commitment with a *call to action* that appeals to your client's sense of reason. With this group, decisions follow analysis; therefore your *call to action* should be aligned with this systematic process. At the conclusion of your presentation consider asking, "If you are in agreement with our recommendations, may I suggest we take the next logical step?" By the way, the next logical step may mean setting up the next meeting, getting another party involved, or some other specific course of action. The main thing is that you end the presentation with a specific request to move the process forward.

---

**PRESENTATION TIP:**

**High C's are silently evaluating you
on your level of professional
competence so ensure that you
and everything you produce
are of a high caliber.**

---

High C's are silently evaluating you on your level of professional competence, so ensure that you and everything you produce are of a high caliber.

When you follow these presentation tips to members of this profile group, you align with their decision-making needs and by doing so you accelerate a favorable buying decision.

---

## PRESENTATION ACTION PLAN

---

**O——INSIGHTS:**

**Know** that high C's *desire accuracy of information, fear making a mistake,* and are silently evaluating you on your *professional competence.*

**O——SKILLS:**

**Apply** a presentation strategy that:

- Aligns with the high C's comprehensive *content* needs.

- Aligns with the high C's highly linear *structure* needs.

- Aligns with the high C's logical and consistent *delivery* needs.

> *"A man convinced against his will*
> *is of the same opinion still."*
> – Unknown

# WHERE ARE YOU COMING FROM?

## The GAP

When a sales professional attempts to sell to a client in the opposing behavioral quadrant, and fails to adjust accordingly, the presentation is doomed to fail.

## The BRIDGE

If you've ever traveled to a foreign country without speaking the language then you've found yourself in a similar quandary as when attempting to sell to a client whose buyer profile is opposite of your own.

You connect best with clients who share your same primary behavioral characteristic. High I's sell best to other high I's. High S's sell best to high S's and high C's sell best to high C's. The only sales profile that may encounter resistance when selling within its profile group is the high **D**. High **D**'s sell best to other high **D**'s as long as the sales professional knows when to back down.

Therefore it's safe to say that, based on your **DISC** profile; you naturally connect with approximately 25 percent of your clients.

---

### PRESENTATION TIP:

Based on your DISC profile, you
naturally connect with approximately
25 percent of your clients.

---

Those with similar profiles are a breeze to sell to because they are easily influenced by you. You speak the same language—your *verbal, vocal,* and *visual* communication style is in complete alignment with theirs. They get you, because you get them.

Chances are good you've had this experience before: you've met a client, established instant rapport, uncovered his/ her needs, located the ideal product/ service solution, and secured the business without a hitch. Everything from start to finish was effortless. This is what happens when you're in selling sync.

But you've also likely had the experience in which you were not in sync. Rather than being effortless, everything was effortful. In fact, nothing flowed! This is what happens when you are selling to a client in the opposite behavioral quadrant of your own (ie **D** to **S**, **I** to **C**, **S** to **D**, and **C** to **I**). This condition is referred to as "cross-communication."

Let me give you some insights into the psychology of influence as it relates to contrasting profile groups. This should shed some light on why it's a challenge selling to a client in the opposing quadrant.

When engaged in the sales process:

- **D** sales professionals *influence with* "force of character" while **S** clients are *influenced by* "reasoning skills, trustworthiness, and dependability."

- **I** sales professionals *influence with* "praise, favors, and personal service" while **C** clients are *influenced by* "accuracy, attention to detail, and competence."

- **S** sales professionals *influence with* "determination and consistency of performance" while **D** clients are *influenced by* "strength of personality, power, and an ability to get the task done quickly."

- And finally, **C** sales professionals *influence with* "factual data and logical argument" while **I** clients are *influenced by* "an inspiring message combined with the strength of relationship."

Can you see a bit of a problem here? The ability to influence does not naturally extend beyond behavioral boundaries. And that's just part of the problem—here are some other mistakes sales professionals make when presenting to buyers in their opposite behavioral quadrant.

**D sales professionals selling to S clients:**

When presenting to S clients, D sales professionals focus on the *outcome* rather than the *relationship*. They get right to the point rather than taking the time to listen and uncover hidden fears or concerns. They speak with a *louder* volume, *quicker* pace, and more *businesslike* tone than preferred by the high S client. This misaligned sales strategy results in buyer anxiety.

**I sales professionals selling to C clients:**

When presenting to C clients, I sales professionals fail to provide the logical data to support the client's decision-making needs. Instead of following a linear and logical presentation format, they tend to wing it and rely on their quick wit and recovery skills to carry them through. In addition, they speak with a *faster* pace, a *louder* volume, and a more *enthusiastic* tone than as preferred by the high C client. This misaligned sales strategy results in buyer frustration.

**S sales professionals selling to D clients:**

When presenting to D clients, S sales professionals speak using a *softer* and *less direct* communication style. They follow a much longer presentation format than required by the high D to make a buying decision. They also speak with a *slower* pace and *lower* intensity, and from a *more collaborative* perspective, than as preferred by the client. This misaligned sales strategy results in buyer frustration.

**C sales professionals selling to I clients:**

When presenting to I clients, C sales professionals rely more heavily on factual data; follow a more linear structure; and speak with a *slower* pace, *lower* intensity, and with *less engagement* than as preferred by the high **I** client. This misaligned selling style results in buyer frustration.

Know with absolute certainty that when a client experiences the emotions of *anxiety, frustration,* or *resentment* it does not support a favorable buying decision.

If you, as the sales professional, neglect to adapt your engagement style accordingly, your presentation will fail to align with your client's decision-making needs. Given the choice, your client will overlook you in favor of a competitor whose communication style is better aligned with his/ her own, even if their product/ service offering is an inferior one.

---

## PRESENTATION TIP:

**If you, as the sales professional, neglect to adapt your selling style accordingly, your presentation will fail to align with your client's decision-making needs.**

---

This is where teams or partnerships come in handy. Having two, three, or four people on a sales team is an effective way to respond to differences in buyer profiles. An effective sales team is one that is behaviorally balanced, including elements of Dominance, Influence, Steadiness, and Compliance within the full makeup of the team. With a well-balanced team, you're able to pass the presentation baton over to the team member whose sales profile is best aligned with the client's decision-making needs.

This behavioral matching process will always yield a better result, assuming the client has no other underlying personal or cultural biases negatively influencing his/ her purchase decision.

The only thing left to consider, as it relates to tailoring your content, is what to do when you are presenting to more than one person. This question gets answered in the next Acceleration Strategy.

---

### PRESENTATION ACTION PLAN

---

**○━━INSIGHTS:**

Know that you connect easiest with those who reside within
your own profile group, you connect moderately well with
those in the adjacent profile groups, and you connect least well
with those in the opposite profile group.

**○━━SKILLS:**

Apply an adaptive presentation strategy to align with the
unique decision-making needs of your client.

---

> *"You can say one thing to some people and move them deeply, whereas the same message to others will leave them completely uninspired."*
> – Gerald G. Clerx

# YES, YES, YES ... ABSOLUTELY NOT!

### The GAP

Many sales professionals fail to consider the unique needs of all decision makers and as a result, fail to obtain consensus.

### The BRIDGE

Every sales presentation you deliver is open to individual interpretation. A client's perception of your presentation is filtered by past personal experiences. That's why two people can listen to the same message and have completely different reactions.

As a trainer, every time I conduct a live workshop, it is to a multi-profile audience. In the same room I'll have a full spectrum of DISC profiles, each with their own unique *content, structure,* and *delivery* needs.

My "desired reality" outcome is to satisfy the learning needs of ALL my audience members so that each one leaves having acquired the insights, skills, and resources to accelerate their professional success.

Because I'm an **ID** (Influence and Dominance) profile myself, I connect most easily with my **ID** course participants. Early in my training career I recognized that, while inspiring the **I**'s and **D**'s, I was not connecting as well with the **S** and **C** workshop participants. This misalignment was evidenced by the occasional course evaluation comment that read, "felt too rushed," "more group work needed," or "not enough practical examples."

S and C participants were frustrated by the very thing that the D and I participants loved about the course. It wasn't until I adjusted my content and delivery methodology to meet the needs of all four profile groups that I began to connect with everyone in the room.

That same content and delivery misalignment is occurring in the presentations you deliver to multiple decision makers. You are connecting with some, but alienating others.

Here are three recommendations when making presentations to a multi-profile team of decision makers. Your presentation could be to a high C husband and high I wife; or an executive committee consisting of a high D CEO, a high I COO, and a high C CFO; or a room full of investors covering the whole behavioral spectrum. When confronted by any multi-profile sales situation, consider responding with one of the following strategic approaches:

**Personalize your engagement strategy**

During your presentation, take moments to connect with every person in the room in a way that aligns with his/ her respective engagement needs. The high I and high S profile groups like to be engaged more frequently than the high D and high C profiles groups. Ask high I's for their feedback and ask high S's if they have any questions or concerns. Respond to both accordingly. However be sure not to spend too much time dialoguing with one person because you run the risk of alienated everyone else in the room.

**Provide comprehensive evidence**

Another alignment strategy is to make sure your presentation includes evidence that meets the needs of all key decision makers. Your objective should be to include the appropriate amount of *facts, figures, stories, testimonials,* and *examples* to meet the decision-making needs of the full group. Don't make the mistake of directing your presentation to the individual who you feel is the key decision maker, unless you're sure. It's more likely that all participants will have a say in the final recommendation. In the event you know who the key decision maker is, weight your evidence toward the needs of that person.

**Personalize your delivery of evidence**

Consider custom tailoring the delivery of your presentation by communicating key pieces of evidence directly to the person who needs to hear it, in a way they need to hear it, even if you exclude the other participants for a brief moment. For example, "John, you mentioned to me that return on investment was your primary concern, so I've prepared a comprehensive market forecast to support this proposal, which I'd be happy to leave with you." By the way, that whole statement should be directed to that specific decision maker.

You now know what to say and why, and what not to say and why not. You understand the *content* and *delivery* needs of all buyer profiles and how to align your presentation accordingly, whether one-on-one or in a group setting.

In the next chapter you'll be introduced to a series of presentation techniques and audience involvement strategies that will further accelerate the transaction with sales presentations that are memorable, impact-full, and inspiring.

---

**PRESENTATION ACTION PLAN**

---

**○━INSIGHTS:**

**Know** that individual decision makers have specific decision needs that must be addressed if you are to get a full endorsement of your product/ service offering.

**○━SKILLS:**

**Apply** a personalized engagement strategy when presenting to a group of two or more decision makers:

- Personalize your level of engagement, or

- Provide comprehensive evidence to meet the needs of all decision makers, or

- Personalize the delivery of your evidence.

THE **PRESENTATION** PHASE

~Chapter Six~
# Strengthening Your Delivery

*Accelerate your selling success with presentations that
are memorable and impact-full.*

*"Think twice before you speak, because your words and influence will
plant the seed of either success or failure in the mind of another."*
– Napoleon Hill

> *"If you talk to a man in a language he understands, that goes to his head. If you talk to him in his language, that goes to his heart."*
> – Nelson Mandela

# GRAB ME! HOLD ME! MOVE ME!

### The GAP

Even with the ideal product/ service solution, some sales professionals lack the ability to grab their client's attention, hold their interest, and move them to action.

### The BRIDGE

Now don't get excited—"Grab Me! Hold Me! Move Me!" is not a relationship strategy, it's a presentation strategy and it references the need to *capture attention, maintain interest, and inspire action.*

Reflect on some of the truly great speakers of our past: John F. Kennedy, Eleanor Roosevelt, and Winston Churchill. Each possessed the ability to captivate their audience, hold their interest and inspire them with the strength of their words, conviction, and mannerisms. Now granted, you don't deliver your product/ service offering on the world stage; however the end objective is the same—to inspire your audience to take a specific course of action based on the information presented.

---

### PRESENTATION Tip:

The objective of any sales presentation is to inspire your audience to take a specific course of action based on the information presented.

---

In most cases, it isn't the salesperson with the best product/ service offering that wins the business; it is the one who delivers the most compelling presentation.

Remember, a compelling presentation is a balanced blend of *logical structure, tailored content*, and *inspiring delivery*. Master all three of these and you find yourself in elite company. Many believe it was the combination of these three leadership qualities that propelled Barack Obama's rapid ascent up the political ladder.

We've already addressed *logical structure* in Chapter Four and DISC *tailored content* in Chapter Five. So let's shift our attention to *inspiring delivery* techniques. Keep in mind that every time you step in front of your client, you add impact to your message in one of two ways:

Vocal Emphasis: What the client hears.

Visual Emphasis: What the client sees.

## Vocal Emphasis

Vocal communication is represented by your *tone, pace, volume, rhythm, pitch,* and *cadence,* all of which add nuance to your spoken words. Vary either of these and you change the context of the message's meaning.

Let me give you an example of what I mean by using a simple nine-word statement: "I didn't say I was in love with you." Now granted, this isn't a phrase you would likely introduce in the early stages of a client relationship, but I use it to make a point. The syntax of the message is straightforward, yet the meaning is tied to where the vocal emphasis is placed. Listen to how changes in vocal emphasis result in changes to message context.

- "<u>I</u> didn't say I was in love with you." In this case the inference is that it must have been someone else who said it.
- "I <u>**didn't say**</u> I was in love with you." Here the speaker is denying that he said it.

- "I didn't say **I** was in love with you." In this statement the speaker is suggesting that someone else is— but not him.
- "I didn't say I was **in love** with you." Here the speaker is suggesting that he may <u>like</u> you, but that's the extent of it. And finally,
- "I didn't say I was in love **with you**." This statement suggests that the speaker is in love, but that the object of his affection is someone else.

Five different contextual meanings from one simple nine-word statement!

Vocal *tone, pace,* and *volume* are simple tools that you can apply consciously to create additional impact to your spoken words. Here are some additional vocal emphasis techniques you can use to draw attention to key words and phrases:

### Silent bookends

To increase retention of key words and phrases, use the silent bookend technique, which involves pausing before and after your key point. Now this is important ..................... to add message impact, pause before your key point and then pause again after...................The silent bookend creates a space within the client's mental filing cabinet before and after the key piece of information, which makes it easier for him or her to retrieve when required.

### Repetition

Another way to increase retention of a key point in your presentation is through repetition. Repeat the key word or phrase once or twice during your presentation. I'll say that again: repeat the key word or phrase once or twice during your presentation. Repetition reinforces the critical elements of your presentation and makes them easier to recall.

## *Pace shifting*

When approaching a key word or phrase, slow your vocal pace down. This technique is known as pace shifting and draws attention to a specific segment, or key point, of your presentation. So remember, when you get to the good bits...s l o w......y o u r........... p a c e..........d o w n!

## Visual Emphasis

Visual emphasis will also add the impact to your sales presentation. Here are some of the ways in which you can use hand gestures to reinforce the key points of your sales message:

- *To summarize key points:* **For example,** use one, then two, then three fingers to summarize the three parts of your sales presentation.
- *To redirect your listener's attention:* For example, when pointing out specific text or visuals; however, use open palms when directing attention to another individual. Open hands, palms out is much less threatening than an index finger pointing in the client's direction. In some cultures, pointing at someone may be considered offensive.
- *To provide perspective:* For example, expanding your arms conveys growth, while contracting them might convey a narrowing perspective of a product/ service offering. You could apply this technique when using a divergent formatting strategy introduced in chapter four. For instance: "Here's what's happening statewide or provincially (hands expanded), here's what's happening regionally, and here's what's happening locally (hands contracted)."
- And finally, use hand gestures to convey movement by shifting them from the left side to the right or back to front. For example, "My role is to take you from where you are now (current reality) to where you want to be (desired reality) in order to expand your business."

Now these may seem like subtle distinctions; however, the impact of these visual reinforcement techniques is significant. Adding a visual element to your spoken message will increase your client's retention of your information dramatically—and this comes in very handy when it's your product/ service offering that you want your client to recall when the time comes to make a decision.

Be mindful to apply these techniques purposefully and sparingly. An overuse of hand gestures or vocal impact techniques during a presentation diffuses the impact of your key points. You want your client to be inspired by your message, not distracted by it.

---

**PRESENTATION Tip:**

**Vocal and visual impact techniques
should only be used when you
want to draw attention to what
you are saying.**

---

---

### PRESENTATION ACTION PLAN

---

**O—INSIGHTS:**

**Know** that every message can be enhanced vocally and visually to ensure it *captures attention*, *maintains interest*, and *inspires action*.

**O—SKILLS:**

**Apply** vocal and visual impact techniques:

- To direct the attention of your client to key words or phrases.

- To capture attention, add message impact, and increase long-term retention.

**O—RESOURCES:**

**Refer** to our *Presentation Critique Form* to critique a ten-minute video taped sales presentation of your self. Go to <u>www.theGAPanalysis.com</u> and click on "Resources" page to learn more.

> *"What we hear, we forget. What we see, we remember.*
> *What we do, we understand."*
> – Unknown

# YOU'VE GOT THIRTY SECONDS...
# GO!

**The GAP**

Most sales professionals fail to actively engage their client frequently enough during their sales presentation. As a result, the client becomes distracted or loses interest altogether.

**The BRIDGE**

The average attention span of the North American consumer is thirty seconds, which means active engagement is an extremely important part of any sales presentation. After all, a presentation that does not involve the listener is a lecture, and we all know how enjoyable it is to be on the receiving end of one of those.

Now, your client will not actually tell you that you have about thirty seconds before his/ her mind starts to wander, but the evidence is incontrovertible. Think about it—the average news story, the average television commercial, and the average movie scene lasts no longer than thirty seconds. We have been literally conditioned to remain attentive for thirty-second time intervals. After that our minds tend to drift to topics that we deem of higher interest or a more pressing nature.

During a sales presentation, there are three ways to actively engage your listener:

**Mental Involvement**

Perhaps the best and easiest way to involve your listener is to ask her questions at strategic points of your presentation. Ask *open-ended* questions to gather information and *closed-ended* questions to clarify understanding or to confirm agreement. For those who need a refresher, open-ended questions are those that require more than a one-word response. "What specifically are you looking for?" is an example of an open-ended question.

A closed-ended question seeks a "yes" or "no" response. For example: "So visibility and traffic flow are your two primary leasing considerations, is that right?" Both questioning techniques serve a strategic purpose and should be used accordingly.

A second mental involvement technique is to *request feedback* or *confirm agreement* from the listener. Sample agreement phrases include:

> *Are we on the same page?*
> *Are you in agreement?*
> *Does this seem reasonable to you?*
> *Are we aligned in our thinking?*
> *Is this acceptable to you?*

Not only do these questions involve the listener, they also let you know if your client is still standing by your side on the bridge you've just build for them. By the way, a great time to request agreement is at the conclusion of each part of your three-part plan. Once agreement has been confirmed, you have a green light to proceed to the next part of your presentation.

A third mental involvement technique is to have your client see herself benefiting from your offering. Pictures are far more powerful than words and when the client has a favorable image in her mind, she will be more likely to turn that image into reality.

## Physical Involvement

Now let's look at physical involvement. It was Albert Einstein who said, "Nothing happens until something moves." Granted, he was referencing the theory of quantum physics at the time, but likewise in your presentation it's a good idea to keep your client moving, preferably toward the far side of the bridge. Give your client something tangible to hold on to during your presentation or, if feasible, give her something to experience personally. Examples of physical involvement strategies designed to get the client moving include:

> Food sampling (grocery store)
> Wine tasting (wineries)
> Test-driving (auto dealership)
> Personal fitting (clothing store)
> Personal makeover (cosmetic counter)
> Property showing (residential real estate)
> Property walk-through (commercial real estate)

## Emotional Involvement

Finally, consider involving your prospective client emotionally. This can be a little riskier to accomplish because emotional reactions to identical stimuli will vary from person to person based on personal history. Words or images that inspire a sense of anticipation from one person might elicit anxiety from another. That being said, the safest emotion to elicit during a sales presentation is a feeling of *joy* inspired by relevant and acceptable humor. Humor connects people and stimulates the release of endorphins throughout the body. This naturally fueled feel good chemical is a great way to enhance rapport and reduce buying anxiety.

Make sure, however, that the humor is appropriate to the individual and relevant to the circumstances. Misaligned humor, however innocent, can backfire on you. The profile group most responsive to the use of humor is the high **I**. Other favorable emotions to elicit from this profile group include feelings of *anticipation, excitement, status,* and *acceptance.* High S's respond favorably to stories that evoke feelings of *compassion, collaboration,* and *contribution.*

The high **D** and **C** profiles are not fans of emotional involvement techniques. They're more interested on the rational side of the buying equation.

---

### PRESENTATION ACTION PLAN

---

**O—▪INSIGHTS:**

Know that the attention span of the average North American consumer is approximately thirty seconds and that your client should be frequently engaged (*mentally, physically,* or *emotionally*) throughout the buying process.

**O—▪SKILLS:**

Apply a variety of *mental, emotional and physical* engagement strategies when presenting your product, or service solution to your client.

**O—▪RESOURCES:**

Create your own resource! Prepare a list of appropriate *mental, emotional* and *physical* engagement strategies and integrate them throughout your sales presentation.

> "An effective team consists of a balanced blend of **D**ominance, **I**nfluence, **S**teadiness and **C**ompliance."
> – Gerald G. Clerx

# MEET MY PEOPLE!

**The GAP**

A team presentation represents the ideal opportunity to showcase the collective breadth and depth of expertise, yet few sales professionals know how to deliver an effective team-based presentation.

**The BRIDGE**

The larger and more complex the sales presentation, the more likely you'll require a team of subject matter experts to support your proposal. The team might consist of you, your Managing Director (or Office Manager), a financial analyst, an IT specialist, and/ or others.

Team presentations are remarkably effective when they are well rehearsed and the team members are properly utilized. Here are some guidelines to follow when delivering team-based presentations:

**1. Appoint a team leader**

Every team should have a designated spokesperson. It is the team leader's responsibility to open the presentation, introduce the team, and identify the value each member brings to the project. He or she is also responsible for ensuring that fellow team members don't get drawn off track. The team leader should also be the one who concludes the presentation by *summarizing* the main points and requesting a specific *call to action*.

## 2. Assign individual responsibilities

In a team presentation, everyone involved must be able to clearly articulate his/ her service offering to the client. A service offering is the value that team member brings to the client. "Good morning. My name is Ann Majors and I'm the IT Specialist on this project. My role is to ensure that our technology can be seamlessly integrated into your existing platform."

A service offering is a statement that provides a clear benefit to the client. It tells the client how *what you do* supports *what he or she wants*. Make sure that everyone on your team has a clearly defined service offering and the ability to convey it confidently to the decision maker(s) involved.

## 3. Demonstrate your expertise (without notes)

A great deal of your ability to influence is tied directly to your product and industry knowledge. A client's perception of your expertise is compromised when you're overly reliant on notes or PowerPoint slides to communicate your offering. I once sat through a sales presentation in which the lead presenter read directly from her notes to tell us *her name* and the fact that she brought "passion" to the team. It seemed to me that her name should have been committed to memory by now and that passion is something that comes from the heart, not a script. Use notes as a prompt—not a crutch!

## 4. Give full attention to your team members

Make sure you give your full attention to whoever on your team is presenting. All too often I have observed team members staring at the floor, at the ceiling, or worse yet, out the window, during a fellow team member's delivery. If *you* don't appear to find your colleague's information absolutely riveting, how can you expect *your client* to find it interesting? Everyone deserves your full attention, regardless of how many times you've heard the content before or how dry you find the subject matter. Let your clients witness for themselves that your team is one cohesive unit.

## 5. Check for agreement

At the transition point of each major section of your presentation, stop and check for agreement. It is at these points that you should respond to questions or clarify any misunderstandings. After all, you want everyone on board when you transition into the *summary statement* and *call to action*. Once agreement has been confirmed, introduce the next presenter on your team.

## 6. Watch for visual clues

During your fellow team members' presentations, be conscious of your client's body language. Although not universally consistent, there's a high degree of probability that the following decelerating conditions are present when you observe these corresponding gestures:

> *Disinterest:* Concealed yawns, tapping fingers, easily distracted eyes, and continuous watch checking typically indicate *disinterest* and *boredom*. If you encounter these visual clues, consider pulling in the reigns with a statement such as "Let me get right to the point," and then get right to it.

> *Anxiety:* When your client rubs the back of her neck, raises her eyebrows, tightens a fist or wrings her hands, chances are good she is feeling mentally stressed. If you experience these visual clues, respond with a course correcting statement such as "It seems like you have some concerns that need to be addressed. May I ask what they are?" This query should be enough to elicit what concerns your client needs resolved before reconnecting with your presentation.

> *Frustration:* Body posturing that suddenly closes off or leans away are typically reflections of a person who is emotionally frustrated. Crossed arms, heightened breathing patterns, a reddened face, a more erect posture, and tightened facial muscles are also prominent signs. If either of these signs are

encountered, consider course correcting with a statement such as, "It appears that you have a different perspective on this matter. May I ask what it is?"

Whenever you observe *disinterest, anxiety*, or *frustration* during your presentation: stop, uncover the source, and address it. After all, if your client's core concern does not get addressed he/she won't hear the balance of your presentation.

---

### PRESENTATION Tip:

**If your client's core concern does
not get addressed he/ she won't
hear the balance of your presentation.**

---

### 7. Listen for verbal clues

As I stated in an earlier chapter, the questions your client asks during your presentation will typically reveal her underlying fears, so pay attention. The question "How long have you been selling?" may seem innocent enough, but it is likely rooted in a *fear that you lack the experience* necessary for a project of this scope. "Who is the lead contact in this project?" is likely harboring an *accountability concern*. "This job is too small for a big company like yours" is likely harboring a *fear of falling through the cracks*. "How did you arrive at the total fee?" is likely attached to a *fear of being overcharged*. So pay close attention to the types of questions asked and make sure the underlying fear gets satisfactorily addressed before proceeding.

In chapter eight you'll learn a response strategy known as the **ACRE Formula** ©, which is highly effective at identifying client fears and subsequently alleviating them.

## 8. Anticipate tough questions

You should expect a certain amount of questions to be asked during, or after, a presentation. Here are some tips when responding to client questions:

- *Prepare*: Before you meet with your clients, anticipate the types of questions or objections they're likely to ask and mentally rehearse your responses.
- *Tailor your response*: Match the vocal *pace, tone,* and *volume* of your client. In other words, tailor your response to his or her **DISC** profile. A "straight and direct" question should receive a "straight and direct" answer. A more complex question ought to elicit a more complex response.
- *Own Up*: If you don't know the answer to a question asked, say so and affirm your intent to find out.
- *Confirm the adequacy of your response*: Ask the client if your response effectively addressed his/ her question. If the answer is "yes," carry on. If the answer is "no," ask for additional clarification.

## 9. Be prepared to differentiate yourself

Memorize your response to the statement, "Give me a good reason why we should give the business to you / your team / your company." When a client is having trouble differentiating between product/ service providers, this question will likely get thrown into the mix, and the quality of your answer will tip the decision-making scale in your favor or in favor of a competitor.

Use the GAP Analysis presentation format to provide the most effective response. For example, "There are a number of reasons why our company is the best-positioned organization to help your business achieve its growth objectives" (SOI). Then, using the benefit analysis, go on to provide the client with three differentiators along with a description of how these unique attributes accelerate her success (three-part plan). And when you complete your response, summarize and ask for the business (call to action) because the quality of your response has earned you the right to get it.

## Summary

This concludes the presentation phase of the sales cycle. Assuming you have *tailored your content*, *applied a powerful structure*, and *delivered an impact-full message* then you'll naturally transition into the third and final phase of the Gap Analysis Sales Model ©, the NEGOTIATION phase.

In the next part of this book, you'll discover three sources of negotiating power and learn how to align them in your favor. You'll also discover the three stress sources of every deal, and how to respond to them when encountered. And finally, you'll learn how to recognize and respond to win/lose negotiating tactics and culturally conditioned beliefs.

## PRESENTATION ACTION PLAN

**O——INSIGHTS:**

**Know** that an effective team is one in which all members play a specific role in helping the client achieve his/ her *desired reality* outcome.

**O——SKILLS:**

**Apply** the eight presentation strategies included in this Acceleration Strategy when delivering your next team-based presentation.

## Excellence in Action – PRESENTATION

**The GAP**
Developing a great product is one thing. Getting people to buy it is another story.

**The BRIDGE**
Watching one of Steve Jobs trademark product launch presentations is a lesson in the art of persuasion. Jobs had mastered all three elements of a successful sales presentation; relevant content (what is said); logical structure (how it flows) and; inspiring delivery (how it's said).

Review any one of his product launch presentations and you will see how he skillfully applies the elements of the Gap Analysis Sales Model © in all his product launch presentations. Let me break down his winning formula:

*Part 1 - Define the Gap*
When Jobs begins his product launch keynote presentations he always starts out by making sure everyone understands there's a glaring problem in the market (gap), requiring an innovative solution (bridge). What's interesting about this part of the presentation is that many audience members aren't even aware they have a problem ... until of course, Jobs tells them. The problem is either a missing piece of the mobile device puzzle or an example of product obsolescence in the marketplace. Jobs gift was his ability to spot potential problems well before they became problems and create opportunities well before others could act on them.

In the case of the iPhone product launch, the problem, as Jobs stated, was that the current phones on the market (Blackberry, Nokia etc.) had fixed control buttons that couldn't adapt to new applications. Jobs deftly pointed out that this was a "major problem" and by doing so created an instant gap in the mobile phone marketplace.

## Part 2 - Introduce the Bridge

In this part of the presentation Jobs would introduce (with great visual fanfare) the solution to the problem he had just introduced. This segment always focused on the revolutionary new features and the corresponding benefit the user would experience. The features were always technological marvels and the benefits always pointed toward ease of use or to a new benchmark standard of product design or performance. In the case of the iPhone it was the "bit map screen with multi-touch technology."

## Part 3 – Recommend Action Step

The final part of the presentation was to let you know just how to go about bridging your "latest and greatest" Apple product gap.

## ... And "One More Thing"

Job's made a habit of concluding his product launch keynotes with the phrase "Just one more thing". This statement is the presenter's equivalent of a "free bonus gift." It is a 'value add' statement that leaves audience members feeling like they got a little extra by attending.

On top of all this Steve Jobs had an unbridled passion for the products he developed. That passion was evidenced by his words, his vocal mannerisms and his gestures. On many occasions it seemed almost as through he was about to explode with delight at what he was about to share with his audience. Some of the passionate language he used during his product launch keynotes included:

"This is an incredible device!"

"The iPhone has just reinvented the phone."

"This is really hot!"

"It's unbelievable?"

"It is the thinnest 'smart phone' on the planet"

"People haven't even dreamed about a display like this."

"It's packed to the gills"

"It's the best window on the planet!"

**The Result**

Steve Jobs not only informed his audiences, he engaged and entertained them as well. It was this combination, paired with Jobs obvious brilliance that made him such an effective presenter capable of inspiring millions to take action on his latest and greatest Apple product.

# PART III

# THE NEGOTIATION PHASE

In this part of the book you will learn how to
*strengthen* your negotiating power, *overcome* the
three stress sources of every negotiation,
and *respond* appropriately to tactics
and cultural differences.

# INTRODUCTION TO NEGOTIATION

The third phase of the Gap Analysis Sales Model © is the NEGOTIATION Phase. If the ASSESSMENT Phase "defines the gap" and the PRESENTATION Phase "bridges the gap", then the NEGOTIATION Phase "closes the gap" by transforming the client's *desired reality* into his *current reality*. Think back to the negotiations that you've been involved in during your sales career.

> ➤ Have you ever lost a deal because your client got cold feet or couldn't justify the buying decision?
> ➤ Have you ever lost a deal because, during the negotiation, your client became *anxious, resentful, frustrated,* or *hostile* and walked away from the negotiating table?
> ➤ Have you ever lost a deal because both negotiating parties became positional regarding price, dates, terms, or conditions of the agreement and you were unable to resolve the differences?

If you answered "yes" to any of these questions, then you've suffered the consequence of a failed negotiation.

The NEGOTIATION phase begins the moment a successful presentation has concluded. The moment a client decides to take action on your product/ service offering, the negotiation has begun and concludes only when the product has been delivered or services rendered and full payment has been received. This time frame can span a period of seconds, minutes, hours, days, or even months depending on the type of your offering.

The reason why this sometimes-expansive time period is still considered the NEGOTIATION phase is because the deal is still technically open to rescission. During this transaction period, something could prompt the client to walk away and collapse the deal. The good news is that there are only three conditions that will cause a deal to fail once it enters this phase. When you can competently respond to these three potential deal-breaking conditions, you take control of every negotiation.

Understand that in the NEGOTIATION phase, you are participating in either of two roles: *process facilitator* or *problem solver*. The role of the *process facilitator* is to simply facilitate the natural evolution of the deal, to draw up the agreement, to oversee terms and conditions, to help remove subjects, to consult with planners, to arrange for delivery dates, to deliver signed agreements, to secure deposits, to handle fund transfers, and/ or whatever else is required of you. Your involvement is simply to direct the flow of a naturally evolving process.

Your fee is truly earned when you are engaged in the role of *problem solver* addressing the obstacles and hurdles (stressors) that decelerate the client's forward momentum. While a modest amount of stress is considered healthy in a negotiation, too much of it can bring a deal to its knees. Your role is to ensure that both parties remain standing, walking, and talking.

This part of the book is devoted to providing you with the *insights, skills, and resources to strengthen your negotiating power, overcome the three stress sources of every negotiation, and respond appropriately to tactics and cultural differences.*

In chapter seven I will introduce you to the three power sources of every negotiation: **Attitude, aptitude,** and **action. Attitude** refers to *what you think,* **aptitude** refers to *what you know,* and **action** refers to *what you do.* The **attitude, aptitude,** and **actions** you bring to the table will either accelerate or decelerate the forward momentum of the deal.

The good news is that you control the development of each one of these negotiating assets. *You* control what *you* think, *you* control the amount of information *you* acquire, and *you* control the skills *you* bring to the negotiating table. When you align these power sources in your favor, you'll convert a great number of stalled negotiations into successfully concluded transactions.

In this section, you'll discover the impact your thoughts and beliefs have on a negotiation. You'll also discover the knowledge you need to acquire and the actions you can take to enhance the likelihood of a successful outcome.

In chapter eight I will identify the three negotiating obstacles that can stall the forward momentum of a transaction. These decelerating conditions are known as *mental, emotional,* and *positional stress.*

Mental stress refers to client *fears;* emotional stress refers to feelings of *anxiety, frustration, resentment,* and *hostility*; and positional stress refers to differences in *wants* and *needs.* The critical point to understand here is that if either of these conditions is left unresolved, you end up with a deadlocked negotiation.

In this section you'll learn how to recognize the type of stress present, identify its root cause, and resolve it using a four-step strategy known as the **ACRE Formula** ©.

In chapter nine, you'll be introduced to the eight most commonly applied win-lose negotiating tactics. Although I don't endorse the use of these tactics, I do recommend you become familiar with them so that you can effectively diffuse them when encountered. A win/lose tactical approach is contrary to the win/win philosophy of the Gap Analysis Sales Model ©.

In this section you'll also discover how culturally conditioned beliefs and values can influence the outcome of a cross-cultural negotiation.

In summary, the biggest mistakes sales professionals make during the NEGOTIATION phase of selling are:

- They fail recognize and alleviate *mental* stress.
- They fail to recognize and neutralize *emotional* stress.
- They fail to recognize and resolve *positional* stress.

The Acceleration Strategies that follow will bridge these competency gaps by providing you with the tools to master the core skill of NEGOTIATION.

~Chapter Seven~

# Aligning Your Power Sources

*Accelerate your selling success by recognizing and aligning three negotiating assets.*

*"Win-win is a belief in the third alternative.
It's not your way or my way; it's a better way."*
– Stephen Covey

# ATTITUDE, APTITUDE & ACTION

## The GAP

Sales professionals have enormous influence over the outcome of a negotiation, yet they fail to realize the sources of their negotiating power, and as a result neglect to align them in their favor.

## The BRIDGE

Your effectiveness during the NEGOTIATION Phase of selling can be traced back to three professional attributes. I refer to these as the three negotiating power sources. They are: **Attitude, Aptitude,** and **Action.**

## ATTITUDE

*"Our attitude is the crayon that colors our world." – Allen Klein*

Your attitude is a reflection of your beliefs and thoughts. Understand that your thoughts have a powerful effect on the outcome of any negotiation. After all, your *thoughts* lead to *feelings,* your *feelings* create *emotions,* your *emotions* inspire *actions,* and your *actions* determine *results.* Your *results,* therefore, are a product of the *thoughts* that inspired them.

---

### NEGOTIATION TIP:

Your thoughts have a powerful effect
on the outcome of any negotiation.

---

Let me give you an example of what I mean. Do you know people who seem to have everything go their way? They remain positive even in the face of adversity. They say things like "It'll all work out" or "We'll figure something out"—and they always do. They have a great attitude toward life, business, and others. They have an energy about them that makes you feel great and you find yourself seeking them out just to be in their presence.

On the flip side of the coin, do you know of people who whenever you're around them, they seem to suck the life energy right out of your veins? They don't see the good in any situation and they complain about *everything* and *everybody* to *anyone* who will listen. Everything seems to go wrong for these people. They are harbingers of ill health and recipients of continual and on-going misfortune.

These two contrasting life circumstances can be traced back to the collective thought patterns of each individual. Give them a *checkup from the neck up* and you'll discover that each harbor latent thoughts and beliefs that give rise to their current situation. In essence, they are creating their own external realities based on their internal thoughts. I know this is heady stuff, but I want you to understand the importance of the power of your attitude.

"As a man thinketh, so he becomes." said Greek philosopher Marcus Aurelius in 180 AD. This insight speaks to the universal law of manifestation. Skilled negotiators recognize the power their thoughts have during a negotiation and have developed attitudinal beliefs that support them, regardless of how challenging the other person or the current situation. These supportive core attitudinal beliefs are:

### I am response "able"
Skilled negotiators *believe* that they alone choose their response to any given situation, and they choose responses that support them in achieving consensus.

### *I am opportunity minded*

Skilled negotiators *believe* that every situation and event serves them in some ways, even though it might be difficult to recognize at first. They understand that within every problem there resides a seed of opportunity, and this belief illuminates even their most challenging situations.

### *I am outcome focused*

Skilled negotiators *believe* in the premise that it is wise to focus on exactly what they want, rather than what they don't want. A vision of a positive, collaborative outcome is the only thought they will entertain throughout the negotiating process, regardless of what they encounter. They know the importance of positive visualization.

Perhaps no one epitomized this core belief system better than Thomas Edison, who during his quest for incandescent light, was asked by a reporter if he thought he was a failure for having been unsuccessful in over two thousand attempts to create the world's first carbon filament light bulb.

His response was: "I don't see it as failure at all. I see myself as having discovered over two thousand ways in which one cannot make a carbon filament light bulb. I see myself as two thousand steps closer to my goal." Thomas Edison's response was a reflection of his brilliant **attitude**. He was *response "able"*, *opportunity minded*, and *outcome focused*. He succeeded in bridging the "incandescent light" gap a short time later.

When engaged in a negotiation, be mindful of your thoughts. After all, positive outcomes are difficult to achieve when you are wallowing in a sea of doubt or self-pity.

## APTITUDE

*"All negotiations tip in favor of the person who has the most knowledge."*
– Unknown

Aptitude represents the second source of negotiating power. It refers to the knowledge you possess regarding the critical elements of every negotiation. They are:

### Client aptitude
Obviously, the more you know about your client's product/ service gap, the better positioned you are to bridge it. Your knowledge regarding the client should include awareness about his/ her current situation (current reality), key business objectives (desired reality) and key motivators (fears and desires),

### Product aptitude
It also stands to reason that the more you know about your specific product/ service offering and various options available, the more likely you'll be able to provide the ideal bridge to the client's gap.

### Industry aptitude
Finally, the more you know about the trends affecting your client's business, including financial and technological considerations, the more effective you will be at helping your client get what she wants in life.

When you enter a negotiation complete with a positive **attitude** and a strong **aptitude,** you align two of your three negotiating power sources and accelerate the client engagement process.

---

## NEGOTIATION TIP:

When you enter a negotiation with
a positive attitude and a strong
aptitude, you align two of your three
negotiating power sources.

---

# ACTION

*"If you always do what you've always done, you'll always get what you've always gotten."*
– Anonymous

**Action** is the final negotiating power source and refers to your negotiating skill set. This is the gap that I will bridge in the following chapters.

## NEGOTIATION ACTION PLAN

**INSIGHTS:**

**Know** that your negotiating power can be measured by the focus of your *thoughts* (**attitude**); the depth of your *knowledge* (**aptitude**); and the caliber of your *skill* (**actions**).

**SKILLS:**

**Apply** the following negotiating attributes:

- An attitude of *being responsible, opportunity minded,* and *outcome focused.*

- Knowledge regarding the *client,* the *industry* and your *product.*

**RESOURCES:**

**Create your own resource!** Set an alarm to go off at random times throughout the day and give your self a "check up from the neck up." Are you looking for *what's right* or *what's wrong?*

~Chapter Eight~

# Resolving Negotiating Stress

*Accelerate your selling success by recognizing and resolving the three negotiating stress points.*

෬෧

*"You can't shake hands with a clenched fist."*
– Indira Gandhi

> *"Speak when you are angry – and you'll*
> *make the best speech you'll ever regret."*
> – Henry Ward Beecher

# THREE TITANIC DEAL BREAKERS!

**The GAP**

Very few sales professionals are competent at recognizing the sources of negotiating stress and taking the appropriate **Action** to resolve them. The result is that doable deals are left undone.

**The BRIDGE**

The three sources of potential deal breaking stress are *mental stress, emotional stress,* and *positional stress.* When either of these conditions exists in a negotiation, your role, as the sales professional, is to recognize it, manage it, and then resolve it.

When you can competently respond to these three decelerating conditions, you take control of every negotiation you are involved in and will rarely, if ever, lose a deal. Let's drill down into each one of these stress sources.

## MENTAL STRESS

*"It is a luxury to be understood." – Ralph Waldo Emerson*

Mental stress is the first potential deal breaker. It is the condition that exists when a client's fears of taking action become stronger than her desire for the product/ service itself. In an earlier Acceleration Strategy I asked you if you'd ever lost a deal to a client who suddenly got cold feet and couldn't justify the purchase decision. This is an instinctive buyer response when under the influence of mental stress, a condition that has compelled a number of qualified buyers to walk away from deals they should otherwise have transacted.

---

## NEGOTIATION TIP:

In any negotiation there are three
potential deal breakers:
*mental* stress, *emotional* stress,
and *positional* stress.

---

Fear is a powerful decelerator and can be triggered by a number of external conditions including changing economic times, market uncertainty, third party opinions, lack of trust, or a number of other catalysts. By the way, whose job is it to monitor and manage the client's level of mental stress? I hope you recognize it to be yours, because you'd be right—**IT'S WHY YOU GET PAID!**

## EMOTIONAL STRESS

*"Discussion is an exchange of knowledge; argument is an exchange of emotion."*
– Robert Quillen

Emotional stress is the second potential deal breaker. This form of stress exists when a party to the negotiation gets emotionally worked up and refuses to move off his/ her position or disengages entirely. When I asked you at the beginning of the chapter if you'd ever lost a deal to a client who became *anxious, resentful, frustrated,* or *hostile* during the negotiation? **That's emotional stress!**

When clients state, "I already have an existing relationship with one of your competitors!" they are experiencing emotional *anxiety*. When clients lament, "you've got to be kidding me!" they're experiencing *frustration*. When clients respond to your proposal with "Your fees are way out of line," they are experiencing *resentment*. When a client says, "This is an absolute waste of my time," they have elevated into feelings of *hostility*.

Unfortunately, while under the influence of an emotionally charged state the judgment process gets clouded. It has been proven that the quality of one's decision is directly linked to his/ her emotional stress level. When stress-free, sound business decisions are made; when stressed, poor decisions are made.

Whose role is it to manage the emotional climate of a negotiation? Yes, that's right! **IT'S YOURS! … IT'S WHY YOU GET PAID!**

## POSITIONAL STRESS

*"Diplomacy is the art of letting someone else have your way."*
– Daniele Vare

Positional stress is the third potential deal breaker. This condition exists when two parties to a negotiation cannot reach consensus on the *price*, *dates*, *terms*, or *conditions* of the agreement. A buyer who is not willing to come up to a seller's asking price or accept the vendor's delivery schedule is locked into positional stress.

Unfortunately, once battle lines are drawn, those standing behind those lines often become entrenched; and if the situation isn't properly managed, a deadlock will ensue.

When encountering any stressful situation, our human instincts tell us to respond with either an equalizing counterforce or a withdrawal from the environment. Famed researcher Hans Selye called it the "fight or flight" syndrome. It is this habitual response that may actually kill an otherwise salvageable deal.

Let me give you an example of how our instincts dictate our response to stress. During my live training workshops, I invite a participant to the front of the room and ask that person to face me, extending his right hand toward my chest. I begin to push on the person's hand, gently at first, then more assertively. By doing so I am subtly introducing stress (in a physical form) into his personal space. How do you think the volunteer reacts? You'd be right if you said he responds with an equal amount of counter force. As I increase my force, he increases his. Why does he do it? Because it's what his instincts tell him to do! His instincts override other available response options such as allowing me to push while leading me around the room or dropping his hand suddenly, causing me to fall to the ground. Likewise when clients feel pushed they fight the deal or disengage altogether.

So, whose job is it to recognize and resolve positional stress? Right again! **IT'S YOURS! ... IT'S WHY YOU GET PAID!**

## JAWS OF DEFENSE

*"One of my problems is that I internalize everything. I can't express anger. I grow a tumor instead."*
– Woody Allen

When confronted by mental, emotional or positional stress in a professional setting, unskilled sales professionals typically react with one of four defensive response strategies. I refer to these instinctual responses as the "**JAWS** of Defense."

**JAWS** is an acronym in which "**J**" stands for Justify, "**A**" for Accuse, "**W**" for Withdraw, and "**S**" for Sarcasm.

**J**ustify refers to an attempt to legitimize why actions were taken or why they weren't taken. Examples of justification responses include:

> "Well I did that because…"
> "That is not what I meant."
> "There was no way for me to anticipate what would happen."

Accuse refers to the assignment of wrongdoing to the other, or a third, person. Examples of accusatory responses include:

> "Perhaps you should have been a littler clearer in your request."
>
> "If your secretary had forwarded the signed documents earlier, we wouldn't be having this problem."
>
> "Your purchasing agent should have thought of that before he agreed to the delivery schedule."

Withdrawal is defense by retreat, like the person who walks away from a deal out of fear, frustration, or sheer exhaustion. Examples of withdrawal responses include:

> "It's the best delivery date I can promise you. If it's not acceptable, you'll have to go elsewhere!"
>
> "If you aren't prepared to come up in price, you'll lose this deal,"
>
> "Look, why don't you call me when you are ready to make a serious offer!"

Sarcasm is the final response strategy. It is a blend of one part accusation and one part insult disguised as humor. Although typically reserved for industry colleagues rather than clients, its impact can be equally devastating. Examples of sarcastic responses include:

> "This sales advise coming from a person who hasn't done a deal in three months!"
>
> "I might find that offensive, if your opinion mattered to me!"
>
> "Look who suddenly became the expert, in **MY** market!"

Rest assured that none of these **JAWS** responses will do anything to resolve the existing stress. In fact they have the opposite effect; they exacerbate the problem and further perpetuate the stress.

Think about *your* natural response habit when confronted by a stressed client. Do you find yourself launching into Justification, Accusation, Withdrawal, or Sarcasm? Or are you one of the gifted few who have mastered a singular response that offends equally on all four levels?

No need to feel bad about it—after all, to defend, as we learned, is human nature. The opportunity presenting itself, in that moment, is to recognize when you are locked in the **JAWS of Defense** and upon doing so, stop and choose a non-defensive response strategy—the **ACRE Formula** ©—in its place (more on this later in the chapter).

---

## NEGOTIATION ACTION PLAN

---

**O—INSIGHTS:**

**Know** that there is the potential for *mental, emotional* and *positional* stressors inherent within every negotiation, and that it's human nature to respond with the **JAWS of Defense** when confronted by either of them.

**O—SKILLS:**

**Apply** non-defensive communication skills when confronted by negotiating stress and refuse to Justify, Accuse, Withdraw, or become Sarcastic.

# WHAT ARE YOU *THINKING?*

### The GAP

Most sales professionals fail to recognize when the client begins experiencing "mental stress." By failing to respond accordingly, they lose the deal to buyer's remorse.

### The BRIDGE

Think back over the course of your sales career. How many times have you heard a client respond to your proposal with "Leave it with me," "Let me think it over," or "I'll call you when I'm ready to make a decision"? What the client is really saying in each of these cases is; "your presentation has left me more anxious than desirous of your product/ service offering."

Once again, the Gap Analysis Sales Model © defines "mental stress" as the condition that exists when a client's fears of taking action becomes greater than his desire for product/ service ownership. When this occurs, the transaction will stall and not regain momentum until those fears are identified and subsequently removed.

### Recognizing Mental Stress

Mental stress is easy to recognize when you know what to look for. Its presence is communicated *verbally* through words and phrases, *vocally* by changing volume and tone, and *visually* by hand gestures and facial expressions.

Verbal clues are the most obvious and are reflected in the types of questions a client asks. Here are some indicators that your client's forward momentum has stalled out due to mental stress.

Questions asked include:

- How much time are you going to spend on my project?
- How do you guarantee your work?
- What are some case studies that prove you can do this?
- What other projects has this team worked on in the past?
- What is your fee and how do you justify it?

Statements made include:

- I'm not familiar with your company.
- You sound like everyone else.
- Your fee seems high.
- It looks to us like you have too many projects on the go.
- We are too small for a big company like yours.

Mental stress can also be detected vocally. When your client experiences fear his vocal qualities shift; vocal *pitch* elevates, vocal *tone* turns more businesslike and vocal *pace* quickens. Remain alert to sudden changes in either of these vocal patterns.

Visually, mental stress is also easy to recognize. When in this state a client's brow may furrow, jaw may tighten, head may shake from side to side, fingers may tap nervously, spatial requirements may expand, and direct eye contact may lessen. It is noteworthy that, in most cases, these vocal and visual shifts occur at a totally subconscious level.

Law enforcement officers have long known about the revealing nature of vocal and visual communication and have been tuning in to them for years as a quick test to determine the presence of anxiety. Drive up to any border crossing station between Canada and the US, and you'll likely encounter the same five questions, regardless of your entry point.

This questioning strategy is designed to establish an early "honesty benchmark" from which to compare against. Here's how it works. The first three to four questions are intended to elicit honest responses. These questions typically include: "What is your nationality?" "Where are you headed?" "How long will you be gone for?" and, "What is the nature of your visit?" These are known as *benchmark questions* because their purpose is to establish how you look and sound when you're telling the truth.

The fifth question, however, definitely has consequences attached to it. It's called the *kicker question* and it usually sounds something like, "Do you have any drugs, alcohol, or weapons to declare?"

This is where any subconscious shifts in your vocal and visual communication patterns will disclose whether or not you have something to hide. Breaking eye contact; tapping your steering wheel; clearing your throat; shifting your vocal pace, tone, pitch, or volume; changing your facial expression, or developing an uncontrollable facial twitch in response to this final question is reason enough to direct you toward a second-tier screening process.

So, in all your future negotiations, remain alert to verbal, vocal, and visual clues that might indicate your client is experiencing mental stress. A second thing to consider is that underneath mental stress are the core concerns that support it. Core concerns are almost always expressed as fears; fear of overpaying, fear of making a mistake, fear of change, fear of the unknown, fear of failure etc.

The only way to overcome a client's underlying fear is with the evidence, action plan, or performance guarantee that alleviates it.

### Evidence

The **first** way to overcome mental stress is with evidence. Evidence takes one of three forms: *statistics* (facts and figures), *case studies,* and *testimonials*. Any of these forms of evidence, assuming they address the client's underlying fear, will effectively alleviate his state of *mental stress*.

### Action Plan

The **second** way of overcoming mental stress is with an action plan. An action plan is anything you agree to do or suggest your client do to alleviate his fear of taking action. Due diligence is an example of an action plan.

### Performance Guarantee

The third way of overcoming mental stress is with a performance guarantee. A performance guarantee says, "This is what I promise and here is what happens if I fail to deliver."

Supplying the right evidence, promising to take a specific course of action or making a guarantee of performance, removes fear and allows the client to move forward with confidence.

In all your future negotiations, remain alert to the *verbal*, *vocal*, and *visual* clues that might indicate your client is mentally stressed. If detected, respond accordingly by using a four-step resolution strategy known as the **ACRE Formula** ©, which you'll be introduced to in an upcoming Acceleration Strategy.

---

## NEGOTIATION ACTION PLAN

---

**O⸺INSIGHTS:**

**Know** that mental stress is expressed *verbally, vocally,* or *visually* and if left unresolved will result in a negotiating stalemate.

**O⸺SKILLS:**

**Apply** the following observation techniques to determine if your client is mentally stressed:

- Pay attention to verbal communication patterns such as *words used, questions asked,* and *statements made.*

- Pay attention to vocal communication patterns such as *pace, tone,* and *volume.*

- Pay attention to visual communication patterns such as *body posture, hand gestures,* and *facial expressions.*

**O⸺RESOURCES:**

**Refer** to our list of the statements of mental stress to help you prepare for your next negotiation. Go to www.theGAPanalysis.com and click on the "Resources" page to learn more.

> *"The real art of conversation is not only to say the right thing in the right place, but to leave unsaid the wrong thing at the tempting moment."*
> – Dorothy Nevill

# HOW ARE YOU *FEELING?*

### The GAP

Most sales professionals fail to realize when their client is locked into a state of "emotional stress" and therefore miss the opportunity to resolve it.

### The BRIDGE

The Gap Analysis Sales Model © defines "emotional stress" as the condition that exists when a client experiences *frustration, resentment, anxiety,* or *hostility* during a negotiation. When these emotions are present in a negotiation, the transaction will stall and not regain momentum until the root source of the emotion has been identified and addressed.

---

### NEGOTIATION TIP:

When emotional stress is present
in a negotiation, the transaction
will stall and not regain momentum
until the root source of the emotion
has been identified and addressed.

---

## Recognizing Emotional Stress

Just like mental stress, emotional stress is very easy to spot. Its presence in a negotiation can also be observed by your client's verbal, vocal, and visual communication patterns.

Verbally, the types of statements made and questions asked evidence your client's level of emotional stress. Here are some examples that might indicate your client is in an emotionally stressed state:

Statements made include:

- Your fees are way out of line!
- We had a bad experience with one of your people and don't plan on using you again.
- We have a strong relationship with one of your competitors.
- I don't like using sales agents.
- This offer is insulting.
- What are all these extra fees? Shouldn't they be included in the purchase?
- I've been on hold for 20 minutes!

Questions asked include:

- Why haven't you returned any of my phone calls?
- How much longer is this going to take?
- Why wasn't I told about this earlier?
- What's the hold up?
- Why on earth is this taking so long?

Vocally, an emotionally charged state is evidenced by an increased vocal *volume*, an accelerated vocal *pace*, and an abrupt vocal *tone*.

Visually, signs of an emotionally charged state include reddening of the face, intensified facial expression, spatial intrusion, more erect body posture, heightened breathing patterns, and more directional and assertive hand gesturing.

Once again, the core emotions underlying this form of stress are *frustration*, *resentment*, *anxiety*, and *hostility*. This condition, left unresolved, has the potential to kill the deal and compromise the relationship. Gandhi was right when he said, "You can't shake hands with a clenched fist."

The quality of one's decision is linked to his/ her level of emotional stress. The phrases "I'm out of here!" "You're fired," "Take it or leave it," plus a few other choice words and phrases are all easily uttered while in the grip of a highly charged emotional state.

While mental stress is rooted in fear, emotional stress grows out of perceptual beliefs. The statement "We had a bad experience with one of your people and don't plan on using you again" relates to a belief about something that a person did or failed to do.

The statement, "This offer is insulting!" is *frustration* rooted in a belief regarding the perception of value. The statement "You have a competitive listing in the market" is *anxiety* that stems from the belief that a competing listing will somehow undermine the client's outcome. The statement "I don't like sales people!" could be *resentment* rooted in a belief that sales people are not worth the fee attached to their services.

Just like mental stress, emotional stress must be addressed and resolved. Your instincts may compel you to defend your actions, when the proper course of action is to remain non-defensive and allow the client to fully express herself, regardless of how hard it is to swallow what's being dished out. This can be a difficult undertaking, especially if you feel the comment is unjustified. Emotional stress only begins to dissipate once the stressed client realizes she is being listened to non-defensively.

In all your negotiations, remain alert to the *verbal*, *vocal*, and *visual* clues that might indicate your client is emotionally stressed. If observed, respond accordingly by using non-defensive listening skills to uncover and resolve the root cause using the **ACRE Formula** © resolution strategy.

## NEGOTIATION ACTION PLAN

**O━━━INSIGHTS:**

**Know** that emotional stress is communicated *verbally*, *vocally*, and *visually* and that if left unresolved will result in a negotiating deadlock.

**O━━━SKILLS:**

**Apply** the following observation techniques to determine if your client is emotionally stressed:

- Pay attention to verbal communication patterns such as *words used*, *questions asked*, and *statements made*.

- Pay attention to vocal communication patterns such as vocal *pace*, *tone*, and *volume*.

- Pay attention to visual communication patterns such as *body posture*, *hand gestures*, and *facial expressions*.

**O━━━RESOURCES:**

**Refer** to our list of the statements of emotional stress to help you prepare for your next negotiation. Go to www.theGAPanalysis.com and click on "Resources" page to learn more.

> *"The best general is the one who never fights."*
> — Sun Tzu

# WHAT IS YOUR *POSITION?*

### The GAP

Most sales professionals fail to recognize when the client is locked in a state of "positional stress." By failing to respond accordingly the deal will reach an impasse.

### The BRIDGE

The Gap Analysis Sales Model © defines "positional stress" as the condition that exists when both parties of a negotiation become positional regarding the *price*, *dates*, *terms*, or *conditions* of a contractual agreement. When this occurs, the negotiation will stall and not regain momentum until the underlying interests are uncovered and a collaborative solution is proposed.

---

### NEGOTIATION TIP:

**When a negotiation stalls due to positional stress, it will not regain momentum until the underlying interests are uncovered and a collaborative solution is proposed.**

---

Verbally, positional stress is easy to recognize by listening to the types of questions asked or statements made by the client. Although positional stress is not always communicated in absolute terms, the phrases "I must have," "I will not," and "I refuse to" are all clear indications that you are toe to toe with a client preparing for battle.

Here are some examples of more subtle statements a positionally stressed client might offer up:

- Your fees are too high!
- I don't agree with your pricing!
- I want to go to market without a contract!
- I want a cancellation agreement!
- We've decided to do the work ourselves!
- We must have delivery by the end of the month, otherwise we'll go elsewhere!

Vocally, positional stress is expressed by an intensified volume and firm tone. Visually, it's most easily recognized by closed body language such as crossed arms, a rigid body posture and resolute facial expressions.

While mental stress is rooted in fear and emotional stress is rooted in perceptual beliefs, positional stress is rooted in a specific interest. The statement "Your fees are too high" might be supported by an *interest* in being treated fairly. The statement "I want a cancellation agreement" might be supported by an *interest* in remaining in control of the engagement process. The statement "We have decided to do the work ourselves." might be supported by an *interest* in obtaining the best possible financial outcome. The question "Are you prepared to cut your fees on this deal?" might be supported by an *interest* in saving money or testing your negotiating resolve.

The most effective way to root out the *interests* underlying a client's position is to reply by asking one of the following clarifying questions:

- Why is that important to you?
- What are you basing your opinion on?
- What specific concern do you have?
- What do you hope to achieve by that?
- Can you help me to understand your objective here?

Now clearly, it's difficult to remain non-defensive in the face of positional adversity. When confronted by a strong defensive position you will feel a strong urge to respond with an equally strong counter defensive position of your own. Resist the urge! Fortifying your position will compel your client to do the same, and once your client gets stuck on position he will become less responsive to invitations of compromise. In the face of adversity it takes far more strength and courage to respond non-defensively than it does to respond defensively.

---

## NEGOTIATION ACTION PLAN

---

**O—⚡INSIGHTS:**

**Know** that positional stress is communicated *verbally*, *vocally*, and *visually* and that if left unresolved will result in a deadlock.

**O—⚡SKILLS:**

**Apply** the following observation techniques to determine if your client is positionally stressed:

- Pay attention to verbal communication patterns such as *words used*, *questions asked*, and *statements made*.

- Pay attention to vocal communication patterns such as *pace*, *tone*, and *volume*.

- Pay attention to visual communication patterns such as *body posture*, *hand gestures*, and *facial expressions*.

**O—⚡RESOURCES:**

**Refer** to our list of the statements of positional stress to help you prepare for your next negotiation. Go to www.theGAPanalysis.com and click on "Resources" page to learn more.

> *"A diplomat is someone who thinks twice*
> *before saying nothing."*
> – Anonymous

# THE ACRE FORMULA ©

### The GAP

When encountering strong resistance to their product/ service offering most sales professionals react defensively rather than respond strategically. This results in an escalation of "saber rattling," which can deadlock the negotiation.

### The BRIDGE

Whenever you *encounter mental, emotional* or *positional* stress, you have a choice to respond either defensively or non-defensively.

---

### NEGOTIATION Tip:

Whenever you encounter *mental,*
*emotional* or *positional* stress,
you have a choice to respond either
defensively or non-defensively.

---

Obviously, the more productive response option, in a relationship-driven business is to respond non-defensively. The **ACRE Formula** © is a non-defensive response strategy that is *hard on the problem* and *soft on the person*. It can easily be applied to all situations of negotiating stress.

**ACRE** is an acronym in which the "**A**" stands for **A**lign. The act of aligning with your client is the equivalent of verbal Aikido, the intent of which is not to oppose force but rather redirect the energy toward a deeper understanding of the problem.

The purpose of the alignment phrase is to position yourself next to the client (metaphorically speaking) after all it's very difficult to fight, or argue with, someone who is "standing by your side."

An alignment phrase can be an *agreement*, *acknowledgement* or *empathy* statement. For example:

> "That's a valid point!" (agreement)
> "I can see you feel strongly about this!" (acknowledgement)
> "I understand your frustration ... I'd feel the same way!" (empathy)

An effective alignment phrase diffuses lingering stress and encourages non-defensive dialogue.

The "**C**" in the **ACRE Formula** © stands for **C**larify. The act of clarifying your client's questions demonstrates that you are remaining non-defensive by "seeking first to understand before being understood." Effective clarifying questions will uncover the root cause of the stress. For example, a person's position might sound like "That's my final offer!" however, the underlying stress source might be rooted in a difference in perceived value (mental stress), feelings of frustration (emotional stress), or financial constraints (positional stress), each of which will require a uniquely different response strategy to resolve. Clarifying questions can uncover the root source of your client's stress. For example:

> "Help me to understand why you feel ... (paraphrase the client concern)?"
> "You seem frustrated. May I ask why?"
> "May I ask what you're basing your decision on?"

In some instances the underlying root cause might be difficult to pinpoint. In this case you might have to ask more than a few clarifying questions before you strike pay dirt. Once uncovered, you're face to face with the *six-hundred-pound gorilla* that stands between you and the deal.

The "R" in the **ACRE Formula** © stands for Respond. Your response must address the root source of the stress. If the client is stuck in mental stress then your response MUST allay his/ her fears with *evidence*, an *action plan*, or a *performance guarantee*. If the client is stuck in emotional stress then your response MUST address the unresolved feeling of *anxiety, frustration, resentment* or *hostility*. If the client is stuck in positional stress then your response MUST be aligned with his/ her underlying *interests*. You will learn more about these response techniques in the next three Acceleration Strategies.

Finally, the "E" in the **ACRE Formula** © stands for Encourage. The purpose of the encouraging statement is to reestablish your negotiation's forward momentum. Sample encouraging statements include:

"Does that seem reasonable to you?"
"Does this adequately address your concern?"
"Does that seem like a fair compromise?"

In essence, the encouraging statement confirms whether the six-hundred-pound gorilla is still standing between you and the deal. If the gorilla hasn't stepped aside, then go back and re-Clarify.

The **ACRE Formula** © is extremely effective at overcoming all forms of negotiating stress because it Aligns the participants, Clarifies the core issue, Responds to the core issue, and Encourages consensus.

So, the next time you find yourself facing opposition (from a client or colleague), resist your defensive instincts urging you to Justify, Accuse, Withdraw, or become Sarcastic and instead remain non-defensive and Align, Clarify, Respond, and Encourage.

Notice that when you make this conscious shift away from defensiveness, you accelerate the client engagement process.

## NEGOTIATION ACTION PLAN

○━━INSIGHTS:

Know that mental, emotional, and positional stress, if left unresolved, will cause a deal to become deadlocked and eventually collapse.

○━━SKILLS:

Apply the **ACRE Formula** © when responding to negotiating stress:

- Align with your client

- Clarify your client's underlying fear, belief or interest.

- Respond with the information required to resolve the stress source.

- Encourage your client to regain forward momentum.

○━━RESOURCES:

Create your own resource! Identify the top ten statements your clients make when they become defensive during a negotiation, and determine whether they are rooted in *mental*, *emotional*, or *positional* stress.

# ACRE Eliminates *MENTAL* Stress

### The GAP

When confronted by a client's state of mental stress, most sales professionals respond to the surface comment rather than confirming and resolving the client's underlying core concern. As a result, the unresolved fears persist throughout the negotiation, decelerating forward momentum.

### The BRIDGE

Remember, mental stress is the condition that exists when a client's fears of taking action become stronger than his desire for your product/ service offering. Causes of mental stress include economic uncertainty, lack of information, lack of product familiarity and lack of trust to name a few. Whatever its root cause, this condition will stall the forward momentum of the transaction and ultimately derail the deal if left unresolved.

Let's take three mentally stressed statements and put the **ACRE Formula** © to the test. Consider this scenario: you are presenting your service offering to a client who looks at you with questioning eyes and states:

### I'm not familiar with your company!

What do your instincts tell you to do? If you're like most, you'd feel compelled to defend the company you represent with something like, "Oh we've been around for years!" (Justification).

Now, Justification of track record may well be required, but not until you Align and Clarify, because at this point you haven't yet established your client's underlying *core concern*.

Using the **ACRE Formula** ©, we would respond as follows:

> **A**lign: Remember, an alignment phrase can be an *agreement*, *empathy* or *acknowledgement* statement. In this case it would be most appropriate to align using an agreement phrase such as, *"It's true that our company is lower profile than our competitors."*

> That's all that is required in an alignment phrase, the purpose of which is to demonstrate that you accept what the client is saying and are not defending against it.

> **C**larify: The next step would be to clarify your client's core concern with as many clarifying questions as required. The obvious clarifier would be *"Do you have some concerns about our ability to handle a project of this scope?"* If the answer is "yes" ask a second clarifier such as, *"In what way?"*

> Let's assume the client is concerned about your *capabilities*.

> **R**espond: Remember, mental stress can only be resolved in one of three ways: *evidence*, an *action plan*, or a *performance guarantee*. Evidence would include facts, case studies and/or testimonials. An action plan would include a promise to perform to an agreed upon work standard. A performance guarantee would be a promise to achieve a specific outcome. In this scenario evidence would more be the most effective response at addressing the client's core concern regarding your capabilities.

> An evidence-based response might sound like: *"Fair enough! Let me show you some other projects our company has worked on*

*that were similar in scope.*" Note: three pieces of evidence are all that is required to alleviate mental stress.

Assuming your evidence was satisfactory, the six-hundred-pound gorilla, nicknamed "lack of project capabilities," should now be effectively sedated. To confirm whether this is the case, take the final step in the **ACRE Formula** © and Encourage the client to move forward.

Encourage: A statement such as *"Do these examples alleviate your concerns regarding our project capabilities?"*
　　　If "Yes": suggest next step
　　　If "No": go back to Clarify

**Let's try another one!** In this case, a client responds to your product/ service proposal with:

## It looks to us like you have too many other projects on the go?

Underlying this statement of mental stress is a number of possible core concerns. Examples include:

- *Fear* of falling through the cracks
- *Fear* of conflict of interest
- *Fear* of not getting the "A Team"

Do your instincts compel you to defend your ability to handle your current workload with a response such as? "We've got plenty of manpower to handle this project!" (Justify) or "We've always carried a heavy workload!" (Justify) or "You know what they say—if you want something done, give it to a busy person" (Justify).

Now while these responses may be based in truth, they might not address the client's underlying core concern, which can only be uncovered by asking a series of clarifying questions. Here is how the **ACRE Formula** © could be applied to identify and resolve the client's core concern:

Align: An acknowledgement response would be better suited than an agreement phrase or empathy statement. Therefore you might respond with: *"It's true we have a number of other projects on the go."*

Clarify: Your clarifying questions should seek to uncover the source of the concern. *"May I ask what specific concerns you have regarding our involvement in these other projects?"*

Let's assume that the underlying core concern is linked to your ability to complete the project in the specified time frame. Now that this core concern has been uncovered, your response had better alleviate this fear.

Respond: An appropriate response might be: *"I can understand your concern. May I tell you how we are able to manage our existing obligations while assuring you an on time project completion?* (Provide action plan or a performance guarantee)."

Encourage: The final step is to encourage the client to move forward in the negotiation. *"Does this alleviate your concern regarding our ability to meet your project completion deadline?"*
    If "Yes": suggest next step
    If "No": go back to Clarify
    Alright, one more example:

### Your fee seems high!

Underlying this statement of mental stress is a number of possible core concerns. Examples include:

- *Fear* of overpaying, in comparison to other service providers
- *Fear of looking bad to senior partners*
- *Fear* of not getting good value

We've all heard this one before, especially in these price-sensitive times. Does your gut tell you to Justify? Resist your instincts and instead apply the **ACRE Formula** ©. Your opportunity to justify the value of your offering will come later, but first Align and Clarify to ensure your response addresses the client's core concern.

> Align: What alignment phrase would you use? Would you acknowledge, agree with, or empathize with the client? In this situation an acknowledgement phrase would probably work best. "*I understand!*" is about the only way you can align with this statement.

> Clarify: Obviously you would want to clarify the client's point of reference, so you might ask; "*May I ask what (or who) you are comparing us to?*" The client's response to this question will provide you with his point of reference. Let's assume the client's point of reference is a lower fee quoted by one of your competitors. This is a valuable piece of information to uncover; after all, if your client can't make a value distinction between you and your competitor then his decision will likely revert to price.

> Respond: Your response had better be able to demonstrate a value difference between you and whomever or whatever you are being compared with. An example might sound like, "*Let me show you why, although our fees are higher than our competitors, the net financial benefit to you far outweighs the difference in fees.*" (provide evidence).

Encourage: An effective encouraging statement might sound like, *"Can you see how our services will yield a better net result for you?"*

    If "Yes": suggest next step

    If "No": go back to Clarify

The **ACRE Formula** © is remarkably efficient at alleviating mental stress but it takes time to master. Remember; Align with empathy, acknowledgement, or agreement. Clarify to uncover the underlying core concern. Respond with evidence, an action plan, or a performance guarantee to allay that core concern; and Encourage the client to move forward.

When you properly apply the **ACRE Formula** © in the presence of mental stress, you regain traction in the negotiation.

---

### NEGOTIATION TIP:

When you properly apply the ACRE Formula © in the presence of mental stress, you regain traction in the negotiation.

---

## NEGOTIATION ACTION PLAN

**○━━INSIGHTS:**

**Know** that mental stress occurs when your client's fear of taking action becomes greater than his desire for product/ service ownership and that your client will only move forward once this fear is alleviated.

**○━━SKILLS:**

**Apply** the **ACRE Formula** © when responding to mental stress:

- **A**lign with your client by *agreeing, acknowledging* or *empathizing.*

- **C**larify the underlying core concern of your client's mental stress.

- **R**espond with the *evidence, action plan,* or *performance guarantee* to alleviate the core concern.

- **E**ncourage your client to move forward.

# ACRE DIFFUSES *EMOTIONAL* STRESS

## The GAP

When confronted by an emotionally stressed client, most sales professionals respond defensively rather than empathically. As a result, they exacerbate an already charged emotional climate and risk losing the client.

## The BRIDGE

Once again, emotional stress is the condition that exists when a client experiences the emotions of *frustration, anxiety, resentment,* or *hostility* during a negotiation. Each one of these emotionally charged states would decelerate the forward momentum of the deal.

Let's select three emotionally charged statements and put the **ACRE Formula** © to the test. Here's the scenario: You've just contacted a client who has a requirement for your product/ service offering. During your conversation the client states:

> **We had a bad experience with your company and don't plan on using you again.**

Underlying this emotionally stressed statement is a number of possible root causes. Examples include:

- *Frustration* with previous non-performance
- *Resentment* over fees charged
- *Hostility* over perceived product/ service misrepresentation

Let's apply the **ACRE Formula** ©:

**A**lign: In this case an empathy response would be the most appropriate: *"I'm sorry you had a bad experience with one of our people."*

**C**larify: The clarifying question that needs to be asked is *"May I ask what happened?"* Now some might consider this to be a dangerous question because it could open up a can of worms. Guess what – the can is already open! The only chance you have to salvage an opportunity is to hear the client out and take the necessary action. If you played a role in the "bad experience" then you may have to own up and make amends. If you were not involved then you may have to offer up a concession or provide a personal assurance that it will not happen again.

Let's assume the "bad experience" was related to a late product delivery. Your understanding of the problem has gotten you a foothold in the door. The quality of your proposed solution will dictate whether that foothold turns into an open door invitation.

**R**espond: When encountering emotional stress, your response should include empathy, an apology or a personal assurance. In this case your response might be: *"We value you as a client and clearly this should not have happened. May I propose that we add a 'delivery guarantee' clause to our agreement to ensure that this does not happen again?"*

**E**ncourage: Finally, the encouraging statement might sound like: *"Would that be acceptable to you?"*
>    If "Yes": suggest next step
>    If "No": go back to Clarify

Let's try another one. In this scenario a residential real estate agent has presented an offer to the seller. Upon review of the offer, she responds with:

**This offer is insulting!**

First off, what underlying emotion is the seller likely experiencing—*frustration, anxiety, resentment,* or *hostility?* It could be either one but it's likely *frustration.* Let's put the **ACRE Formula** © to the test.

> Align: In this scenario would you align with an *empathy* statement, an *acknowledgement,* or an *agreement* phrase? I suggest it would be wise to empathize: *"I understand you're frustrated with this initial offer."*

> Clarify: Your first clarifying question might be: *"What aspects of the offer are you in disagreement with?"* If price is the primary issue, which it likely is, a suitable follow-up clarifier might be: *"What do you think a more realistic offer price should have been?"* A final clarifying question might be, *"What are you basing your opinion of value on?"*

> The answer to this final clarifying question will provide you with the client's "value reference point." Keep in mind that in any negotiation, *perception is reality,* and the better you understand your client's perceptual reference point the more effectively you can respond to it.

> Respond: In this case your response might be to recommend a logical next step. *"Why don't we compile a list of recent transactions to ascertain true market value and prepare a counteroffer that is reflective of our findings. We have nothing to lose."*

Encourage: Your encouraging statement might sound like *"Does that seem reasonable to you?"*
If "Yes": suggest next step
If "No": go back to Clarify

Are you getting the hang of this? Let's apply the **ACRE Formula** © to one final emotionally charged statement.

### I don't like using sales agents!

Now your initial instinct might be to respond with something witty and sarcastic or to justify the value you bring to the table, but resist the temptation and respond using the **ACRE Formula** © instead:

Align: On the surface this emotionally stressed statement might sound a little difficult to align with, especially since the statement minimizes your professional role. But let's set the ego aside and make an attempt at an appropriate alignment phrase. You might respond with: *"Sounds to me like you've had a bad experience with a sales agent in the past."* Although this is an assumption, it will likely ferret out the root source of the emotional stress.

Clarify: While you *cannot* change past experiences, you *can* clarify if there are any lingering resentments. Therefore you might ask, *"Are you concerned that it might happen again?"* Hearing the client out will diffuse any residual resentment she may have and provide you with some insights into the actions you would need to take, or promises to make, to regain the client's confidence. Let's assume that the root cause of her emotional frustration is linked to a bad experience with one of your industry colleagues.

Respond: In this case you might respond with *"I totally understand and while I can't erase the past, I can provide you with a written assurance that this won't happen in our professional relationship."*

Encourage: An encouraging statement might ask, *"Would you be prepared to move forward if we put this guarantee in place?"*
If "Yes": suggest next step
If "No": go back to Clarify

When you apply the **ACRE Formula** © in response to emotional stress, you regain traction in the negotiation.

---

### NEGOTIATION Tip:

**When you apply the ACRE Formula ©**
**in response to emotional stress, you**
**regain traction in the negotiation.**

---

## NEGOTIATION ACTION PLAN

**INSIGHTS:**

Know that the emotional states of *frustration*, *anxiety*, *resentment*, or *hostility* will deadlock a negotiation until the root cause has been uncovered and resolved.

**SKILLS:**

Apply the **ACRE Formula** © when responding to emotional stress:

- Align with your client by *agreeing, acknowledging or empathizing*.

- Clarify the root cause of your client's emotional stress.

- Respond with *empathy,* an *apology,* or a *personal assurance*.

- Encourage your client to move forward.

> *"Our task is not to fix the blame for the past,*
> *but to fix the course for the future."*
> — John F. Kennedy

# ACRE RESOLVES *POSITIONAL* STRESS

### The GAP

When confronted by a positionally stressed client, most sales professionals respond by attempting to negotiate the position rather than uncovering the interests that support it. As a result they end up in a stalemate.

### The BRIDGE

Positional stress represents the one negotiating stress source that is not entirely under your influence to resolve. It is caused by two (or more) mutually exclusive needs.

Remember, beneath all statements of positional stress lies the interests that support it. Let's explore three examples of positional stress and apply the **ACRE Formula** to resolve them:

**Are you prepared to cut your fees on this deal?**

Before we respond to this question, let's identify some of the possible underlying interests:

- An *interest* in saving money
- An *interest* in being treated fairly (matching a competitor's price quote)
- An *interest* in testing your negotiating skills

Now let's resolve it using the **ACRE Formula** ©:

**A**lign: In this case you might choose to align by acknowledging: *"I can appreciate you wanting to secure the best deal possible."*

**C**larify: The follow-up clarifying question might be: *"What did you have in mind?"* Now, you might consider this to be a dangerous question to ask because it seems to imply that you're willing to compromise your fees on this deal. But rest assured that a willingness to hear the client out does not constitute agreement. In fact, you are simply gathering information from which to formulate a response. If your client's request is unacceptable, you can always counter it or decline it altogether. It's entirely up to you.

A subsequent clarifying question might include: *"What are you basing this request on?"* Let's assume the client's underlying interest is "being treated fairly" because one of the competitors offered to cut their fees on the identical product/ service offering. You now have a reference point from which to formulate your response.

**R**espond: In this case your response should be in the form of an interest-based proposal. For instance, *"Here is what I would be prepared to do... (introduce an interest-based proposal.)"*.

**E**ncourage: Finally, you could encourage with *"Is this compromise acceptable to you?"*
    If "Yes": suggest next step
    If "No": go back to Clarify

Let's try another one. Your client asks you:

### Are you prepared to guarantee your results?

Align: *"I can appreciate you wanting this assurance."* (*acknowledgement*)

Clarify: *"May I ask what kind of guarantee you're looking for and why it's important to you?"* You might follow up with a "tie down" such as: *"If we could come to an agreement regarding this issue, are you prepared to move forward?"* Let's assume the client's primary interest was in ensuring there are no unexpected cost overruns.

Respond: Your response should be in the form of a collaborative solution that addresses your client's underlying interests. For example: *"I would be prepared to cap the price for this project if you would you be willing to ... (request a trade-off concession).*

Encourage: *"Would this be acceptable to you?"*
    If "Yes": suggest next step
    If "No": go back to Clarify

Here is a final example. How would you use the **ACRE Formula** © to respond to the positional statement:

### I want the vehicle delivered by the end of the week!

Align: *"I understand!"*

Clarify: *"May I ask why it is so important for you to have delivery by the end of the week?"*

    Client interest: An immediate need for transportation

Respond: *"Given your current situation, I can offer you a loaner vehicle until yours arrives from the factory. This normally takes two weeks. I'll have the shipment expedited, at our cost, so that you have your new vehicle by next Tuesday."*

Encourage: *"Would that work for you?"*
    If "Yes": suggest next step
    If "No": go back to Clarify

Note that an interest-based proposal will not always yield a favorable outcome, but it's up to you to give it a try. There are only two ways positional stress can be resolved: either "win-win" or "no deal." Unfortunately there will be times when you'll invest time to go through this collaborative process only to find out that there's no way to create a "win-win" agreement and you end up with "no deal"! That **can** happen and represents the one reason why a deal could fall apart once it enters the NEGOTIATION phase.

When you encounter positional stress, use the **ACRE Formula** © to **A**lign with the client, **C**larify his underlying interest, **R**espond with an interest-based solution, and **E**ncourage the client to move forward with your proposal.

Initially the **ACRE Formula** © may seem awkward to apply. Like any new skill, it takes time to master. So take the time and commit the formula to memory. Sit around a boardroom table with your colleagues and/ or team members and throw out commonly encountered statements rooted in mental, emotional, and positional stress, then role-play your response using the **ACRE Formula** ©.

It's a far better idea to master the **ACRE Formula** © in front of your colleagues than your clients. Responding to a hostile client by attempting to recollect what the "**A**" in the **ACRE Formula** © acronym stands for won't go very far in neutralizing the situation.

---

## NEGOTIATION TIP:

**It's a far better idea to master the ACRE Formula © in front of your colleagues than your clients.**

---

Keep in mind that negotiations involve more than just responding to mental, emotional and positional stress. A skilled negotiator must also be responsive to negotiating tactics and cultural differences. In the next chapter, you'll learn how to recognize and respond to the eight most commonly used negotiating tactics and discover the impact cultural conditioning can have on a negotiation.

## NEGOTIATION ACTION PLAN

**O⸺INSIGHTS:**

**Know** that positional stress occurs when a client gets stuck on the *price*, *dates*, *terms*, or *conditions* of the agreement and that she will not move forward until her underlying interests have been identified and accommodated.

**O⸺SKILLS:**

**Apply** the **ACRE Formula** © when responding to positional stress:

- **A**lign with your client.

- **C**larify the underlying *interests* supporting your client's *position.*

- **R**espond with a collaborative interest-based solution.

- **E**ncourage your client to move forward.

~ Chapter Nine ~

# Responding to Tactics & Cultural Differences

*Accelerate your selling success by recognizing and responding strategically to tactics and cultural differences.*

∼

*"Win-lose negotiating tactics lead to lose/lose outcomes."*
– Stephen Covey

> *"You can get much further with a kind word and a gun*
> *than you can with a kind word alone."*
> – Al Capone

# OUT OF MY WAY

### The GAP

Many sales professionals fail to recognize obstructive negotiating tactics and respond accordingly. As a result, they unwittingly give up concessions.

### The BRIDGE

Up until now we've focused on the win-win side of a negotiation, in which the purpose is to establish a non-defensive environment from which to create a collaborative outcome.

In this chapter we'll jump over to the other side—the win-lose side, in which the user's intent is to *compete against* rather than *collaborate with* you. I introduce these tactics, not for the purpose of teaching you how to use them against others, but rather to recognize when they are being used against you, so that you can respond accordingly.

Win-lose negotiating tactics can be categorized into two primary groups:

1. Obstructive tactics: An approach in which the user seeks to gain concessions by obstructing (or threatening to obstruct) the negotiating process, and
2. Deceptive tactics: An approach in which the user seeks to gain concessions through the use of deceptive behavior.

In this Acceleration Strategy you'll discover the most commonly used obstructive negotiating tactics, how they are applied, and how to defend against them when encountered.

### The Tactic

The first obstructive negotiating tactic is called the **Time Delay**.

### The Application

This tactic is used to push the other negotiating party against a known deadline. The user of this tactical approach might request a time extension on a subject removal, delay a counter-response, postpone an appointment, or drag on the negotiation by making a major fuss over a minor issue.

This tactic is effective because a person under time pressure is far more willing to offer up concessions. In fact, Pareto's rule of negotiating states that 80% of all concessions are given in the 20% of time that remains in a negotiation. Follow any high profile negotiation and you'll notice that both parties will remain resolute in their demands until a looming deadline approaches. Under time sensitive stress the parties will reconvene and begin offering up concessions in hopes of salvaging a deal.

This is the underlying reason why postal unions threaten to go on strike in November just prior to the Christmas rush, and why most ferry worker unions issue a strike notice just before the summer holidays. They know exactly when the management team will be more willing (read "financially motivated") to offer up concessions.

### The Response Strategy

The obvious rule in any negotiation is to never disclose your deadline. If, however, your time sensitivity does become known and you suspect that your counterpart is using the time delay tactic against you, respond with clear timelines for counter-offers and/ or subject removals. Do not allow your counterpart to stall the momentum of the negotiation in effort to push you against a deadline.

### The Tactic

Another obstructive negotiating tactic is called **Fait Accompli**.

### The Application

This tactic implies that "what is done, is done" and is not open to any changes. Examples include:

- A pre-drafted purchase agreement complete with fixed price, dates, terms, and conditions with no space for any amendments or changes.
- The buying agent who states that he is only authorized to spend X dollars. Any more has to go through a budgeting approval process, which can take months.
- The mortgage officer who provides you with a handsomely drafted mortgage document complete with pre-approved lending rates established by a distant head office.

This tactic is often successful because of the fact that an inexperienced negotiator may not think to question a pre-drafted document or be willing to invest the time or effort to make changes and submit for re-approval.

### The Response Strategy

The best way to counter Fait Accompli is to ignore it, make the desired changes anyway, initial them, and resubmit. An obstructive negotiating tactic is only effective if you believe the obstruction to be real.

### The Tactic

A third obstructive negotiating tactic is called **The Take Away**.

## The Application

This tactic has the user falsely threatening to withdraw from the negotiation. These false threats may sound like:

"If this is the best price you have then I'll seek out another service provider."

"If you can't meet this delivery date, I'll be forced to cancel the order."

"After lengthy deliberation we've decided to do the work ourselves."

This tactic is effective because it instills in you a fear of loss, which is magnified by the amount of time you've invested in the engagement process to date.

## The Response Strategy

The most effective way to counter the "Take Away" is to use the **ACRE Formula** © response strategy. For example, to the statement "If this is the best price you have then I'll seek out another service provider" you might respond with:

> **A**lign: *"I can understand you want the best possible price."*
> **C**larify: *"What price were you hoping to achieve?"* or *"If we could come to a mutually acceptable price, would you agree to keep your business with us?"*
> **R**espond: *"How about if we (offer minor concession)"*
> **E**ncourage: *"Would you be willing to (request minor concession)?"*
> If "Yes": suggest next step
> If "No": go back to Clarify

The **ACRE Formula** © allows you to neutralize the threat of withdrawal and gently guides the user back to the negotiating table.

## The Tactic

A final obstructive negotiating tactic is called **Good Guy / Bad Guy.**

## The Application

This tactic uses a contrasting strategy in which an unreasonable negotiator (the "bad guy") is played off against a more reasonable "good guy." The contrast between the two well-choreographed actors makes the good guy look and sound a lot more preferable to deal with.

This well used tactic, once referred to as Good Cop/Bad Cop, is still commonly used when dealing with more seasoned negotiating teams. Some unscrupulous car dealerships and time-share sales centers still regularly stoop to this technique as a way to pressure a buying decision from an unsuspecting customer.

## The Response Strategy

The best way to counter Good Guy/Bad Guy is to simply call the actors on their charade. A response of "You're not using Good Guy/Bad Guy, are you?" is usually enough to stop their antics.

Keep in mind that obstructive negotiating tactics are used because, in the short term, they often produce favorable results. In the long run, however, they undermine relationships and reduce the likelihood of repeat or referral business.

## NEGOTIATION ACTION PLAN

**O——INSIGHTS:**

**Know** that *obstructive* negotiating tactics seek to win at the other party's expense and that their continued use undermines relationships, personally and professionally.

**O——SKILLS:**

**Apply** a counter strategy to effectively neutralize *obstructive* negotiating tactics.

**O——RESOURCES:**

**Refer** to the response strategies identified in this Acceleration Strategy when you encounter an *obstructive* negotiating tactic.

> *"A lie gets halfway around the world before the truth has a chance to get its pants on."*
> – Winston Churchill

# NOW YOU SEE IT ... NOW YOU DON'T

### The GAP

Many sales professionals fail to recognize deceptive negotiating tactics and respond accordingly. As a result, they unwittingly give up concessions and weaken their negotiating position.

### The BRIDGE

Just like obstructive tactics, deceptive tactics are used with the intent to win concessions at the expense of others. Here are four of the most commonly used deceptive negotiating tactics:

### *The Tactic*

The first tactic is called **Higher Authority**.

### *The Application*

This tactic has the user deferring the final negotiating decision to a nonexistent or nonessential third party. The "Higher Authority" tactic typically sounds like: "Before I can approve this, I need to run it by my partner /my manager /my executive committee (or other)."

This tactic is deceptive in that the "Higher Authority" does not actually exist, or his involvement is not required. When applied as a tactic, the user will return with one final concession request.

### *The Response Strategy*

The most effective way to counter a suspected *Higher Authority* tactic is to preempt its use by starting your negotiation with the question, "Is there anyone else whose approval is required in this decision?" This preemptive strike will effectively discourage the individual from seeking out a higher authority at the late stages of the negotiation. If someone else's approval is required, attempt to bring that individual to the negotiating table.

## The Tactic

Another deceptive negotiating tactic is called the **Red Herring**.

## The Application

By definition, a "Red Herring" is a falsely presented need introduced with the intent to exchange it later for a real concession. It normally involves a request for something that seems out of the ordinary. Examples might include an earlier than normal delivery date, a smaller than usual deposit amount, or a request for an upgrade not normally offered.

The key thing to understand here is that the Red Herring is just a ploy. The concession requested has little or no real importance to the user other than as negotiating leverage. The user is just requesting it for the purpose of exchanging it later. An example of this tradeoff might sound like: "I might be willing to extend my delivery date (Red Herring) if you would be willing to provide me with a few factory upgrades at no extra charge (concession request)." This tactic is effective because it allows the user to create the illusion of being *fair and reasonable* by his/ her willingness to give and take.

## The Response Strategy

Some experienced negotiators anticipate the use of this tactic and neutralize it by bringing their own Red Herrings to the negotiating table. In this case, the tactic is reduced to a ritualistic exchange of basically meaningless concessions.

Another approach is to simply expose and remove the suspected Red Herring in the early stages of the negotiation with a question such as "Is this a deal breaker if we can't get it for you?" By removing the Red Herring early you prevent it from being used at a more strategic point later.

### The Tactic

A third deceptive negotiating tactic is called **The Future Reward**.

### The Application

This tactic involves dangling a tempting *future* carrot in exchange for a *current* concession. An example might sound like: "If you can cut your fees on this deal, I'll make sure we give you first consideration on our upcoming project."

Unfortunately, in most cases, the "Future Reward" fails to materialize and the promise of additional business is quickly forgotten.

### The Response Strategy

The best way to counter this tactic is to either:

1. Politely decline the request (e.g., "I appreciate the offer, however, I'd prefer to stick to our original agreement."),
2. Defer your concession until the future reward materializes (e.g., "I'd consider an arrangement on the upcoming project when it comes to market"), or
3. Agree, but request the agreement be formalized in writing (e.g., "I would be willing to do that if we were to draft a formal agreement clarifying our intentions.")

### The Tactic

A final deceptive negotiating tactic is called **The Nibble**.

### The Application

This tactic involves a late state request for a change of term (or condition) or an additional concession. Examples include:

"Look, we are very close on price but I'm having second thoughts. I'd be prepared to move forward with this deal if you'd be prepared to throw in a piece of your commission." Or,

"I'm ready to move forward on this deal if your manager would pick up the first two lease payments as a final show of good faith."

This tactic traces its origins to the classic McDonald's Nibble: "Do you want fries with that?" It's a well-documented fact that once a buyer makes a primary purchase decision, he or she is more inclined to say, "yes" to secondary requests or invitational add-ons. The auto industry has traditionally relied heavily on the use of add-ons as a way to increase the transactional value of an auto purchase. Paint protection, scotch guarding, undercarriage protection, extended warranties are all examples of classic dealership Nibbles.

### The Response Strategy

The most effective way to counter the Nibble tactic is to politely decline the request or better yet, propose a tradeoff concession such as "I'd be willing to throw in a piece of my commission if you'd be willing to use our services on your next two projects." Just make sure that your trade-off concession request is of equal or greater value.

Win/lose *obstructive* and *deceptive* negotiating tactics are still widely used in many industries; however increased exposure is limiting their continued ability to influence the outcome of a negotiation.

In today's consumer landscape, negotiations should be collaborative rather than competitive, so refuse to resort to these tactics. It is only important that you know them so that you can recognize when they are used against you and respond accordingly.

---

## NEGOTIATION ACTION PLAN

**INSIGHTS:**

Know that *deceptive* negotiating tactics seek to win at the other party's expense and that there use undermines relationships.

**SKILLS:**

Apply a counter strategy to effectively neutralize *deceptive* negotiating tactics.

**RESOURCES:**

Refer to the response strategies identified in this Acceleration Strategy when you encounter a *deceptive* negotiating tactic.

---

> *"I would imagine hell like this:*
> *Italian punctuality, German humor and English wine."*
> — Peter Ustinov

# KISS, BOW OR HIGH FIVE?

### The GAP

Most sales professionals see things *as they are*, not *as the client is*, and in the process become paralyzed by their own culturally conditioned beliefs and values. They base their conduct on their own social mores and by doing so fail to consider any beliefs, or follow any protocol, that they themselves are unfamiliar with.

### The BRIDGE

Effective negotiators recognize that their key to success during a negotiation is tied to their ability to see things *as their client sees it.*

---

### NEGOTIATION Tip:

**Effective negotiators recognize that their key to success during a negotiation is tied to their ability to see things *as their client sees it.***

---

It is from within this client-centric perspective that buying decisions are made and negotiating terms and conditions are justified. In this chapter I will introduce you to some of the preconditioned values and beliefs that you need to be aware of, and responsive to, when conducting business with a client from the international community. These are guidelines only and should not be relied upon exclusively for your success. In some countries there may well exist "intra-cultural" differences that will further influence the strategic approach you would take during the negotiation.

As negotiators, we are strongly influenced by our own paradigms and culturally conditioned belief systems. This preconditioning often keeps us from interpreting cross-culturally communicated messages, as they are truly intended.

The following communication patterns are often misinterpreted when engaged in a cross-cultural negotiation:

## Vocal Patterns

### *Loud vocal volume*

*Intention*: To Americans and Australians, this communication style is intended to convey boldness, confidence, directness, and an eagerness to get right down to business.

*Perception*: Some cultures (e.g., Japanese, Chinese, or English) may interpret a loud vocal volume as offensive, finding the speaker to be overbearing, disrespectful, self righteous and/ or egotistical.

### *Quick vocal pace*

*Intention*: To some cultures, such as the Spaniards, Mexicans, and Italians, a quick vocal pace is intended to convey an appreciation toward you and an enthusiasm toward your product/ service offering.

*Perception*: Some cultures (e.g., Germans, Kiwis, or English) may interpret this behavior as disingenuous, overly emotional and/ or reflective of a person who is not being truthful.

*Monotone voice*

> *Intention*: Germans and Scandinavians often speak with a more serious and monotone voice, which they use to convey logic and reason—two important culturally conditioned decision-making attributes.

> *Perception*: Some cultures (e.g., English, Mexican, or Australian) may interpret this tone as reflecting an impersonal, aloof, or standoffish character.

These misalignments of *intention* and *perception* will result in anxiety, frustration, or resentment, depending on which side of the fence you're seated. In either case, the negotiation may falter based on an incorrect interpretation of your client's intended message. Once momentum is lost, it can be difficult to re-establish.

Now that we've addressed vocal qualities, let's shift our focus to the visual elements of communication. Studies confirm that when two parties are engaged in a negotiation, the majority of the message's meaning is expressed visually. A person skilled at reading body language is at a real advantage in a negotiation, especially if that skill is coupled with an awareness of culturally conditioned *hand gestures, body posture,* and *facial expressions.*

---

## NEGOTIATION Tip:

A person skilled at reading body language is at a real advantage in a negotiation, especially if that skill is coupled with an awareness of cultural conditioning.

---

## Visual Patterns

Here are some insights into the impact of your visual communication (body language) when negotiating with a client from a culture other than your own.

### Hand Gestures – greeting style

To most North Americans, Australians, and Hungarians, a strong handshake conveys strength and confidence; however, the same cannot be said for most Asian cultures. The Chinese and Japanese offer up a far gentler greeting and the South Koreans may not extend a hand at all and instead replace it with a respectful bow. The resultant perception of the first group is that Asians lack strength, while the Asian group interprets an assertive greeting style as a reflection of one lacking in subtlety and grace—two revered behavioral attributes among Asians.

### Hand Gestures – animation

Excessive and animated *hand gestures* are quite common during negotiations within many North American and European countries, but most Asians find the practice of excessive hand gesturing to be offensive, disrespectful, and distracting. East Indians, in particular, will become offended when you point your finger to something or, worse yet, at someone.

### Body Posture

With respect to *body posture* and *positioning,* recognize that physical contact during a negotiation is very common among the Mediterranean and Latin cultures. Mexicans, Brazilians, Italians, and Greeks are particularly well known for their tactile communication style throughout all three phases of the sales cycle. By not reciprocating in a similar manner, you may appear aloof or standoffish to each of these countrymen.

In many cultures (especially Asian), a buffer zone is preferred between the negotiating parties. Not only is physical contact frowned upon, but it may also be interpreted as a sign of disrespect or aggression.

## Facial Expressions

And finally, with respect to *facial expressions*, North American and many European cultures use animated facial expressions to convey emotion. These animated expressions are used to convey feelings of agreement, excitement, enthusiasm, appreciation, and a host of other meanings. This, however, is not the case among the Japanese, Chinese, and Koreans who are far less animated. It's very difficult for most Westerners to read the emotions of their Asian counterparts because their culturally conditioned patterns of expression are far too subtle for them to pick up on.

Head gestures between cultures may also lead to confusion, especially when involving a client from India or Bulgaria, where nodding the head up and down signifies a "No" response and tossing of the head from side to side indicates a "Yes" response.

Before entering into a negotiation with a client from another country, take some time to learn about his/ her culturally conditioned *vocal* and *visual* communication patterns.

## Summary

A skillfully concluded negotiation transitions your client from his/ her current reality condition to his/ her desired reality outcome. The Gap Analysis Sales Model © has been successfully concluded. Your qualified prospect has transitioned into a satisfied client.

The only thing left to do is to take stock of your performance, build on your strengths and learn from your mistakes.

In the next section of this book you will discover a strategy to ensure that your past client becomes a source of future and referral business.

---

## NEGOTIATION ACTION PLAN

---

**O——INSIGHTS:**

**Know** that culturally conditioned values and beliefs strongly influence behavior within a negotiation and that many deals are lost due to cultural ignorance.

**O——SKILLS:**

**Apply** your cultural awareness to interpret vocal and visual communication during a negotiation and align accordingly.

**O——RESOURCES:**

**Refer** to the *Bridging the Cultural Gap* audio series to help you accelerate client engagement in cross-cultural negotiations. Go to www.theGAPanalysis.com and click on the "Resources" page to learn more.

## Excellence in Action - NEGOTIATION

> **The GAP**
> Negotiations cost individuals and organizations time, energy and money.
>
> **The BRIDGE**
> In my mind, the best examples of organizations that have mastered the art of negotiating are Amazon.com, Apple and Costco. Why? Because they don't negotiate! Walk into any Apple retailer or Costco warehouse and try to haggle the price of your acquisition. It's not going to happen!
>
> These organizations have learned that by doing an excellent job at identifying the gaps in the market and then brilliantly executing on building the bridges ... they don't have to negotiate. Their clients are willing to buy their products on their terms and conditions.
>
> As I stated earlier, when a sales organization is really proficient at the ASSESSMENT and PRESENTATION phases of selling, there is nothing to do in the NEGOTIATION phase except direct traffic. In fact, negotiating stress is non-existent:
>
> ➤ *Mental stress* does not exist because of the size, strength and return policies of the organization alleviates any fears or concerns the client may have about acquiring the product in the first place.
> ➤ *Emotional stress* does not exist because any problems or concerns are quickly and non-defensively addressed. It's hard to get frustrated with a company that operates under a 100% customer satisfaction service commitment.
> ➤ *Positional stress* does not exist because the only option available is to do business with them or not. If you do choose to do business, it is on their terms ... not yours. It's hard to become locked in a positional deadlock if there is only one position.

In fact, this is the place that every retailer and service provider strives to attain. An environment in which sales/ service professionals are so well trained at assessing client needs and delivering ideal product/ service solutions that their clients make buying decisions ... without any reservation whatsoever.

The principles of the Gap Analysis Sales Model will take you to a similar place with your business.

**The Result**

The results, for each one of these organizations, speak for themselves in terms of both revenue and customer loyalty.

# After the Deal is Done

*Accelerate your on-going selling success by relentlessly fine-tuning your product/ service offering.*

*Every **past** client is a **current** reference and a **future** prospect!*
– Gerald G. Clerx

# AM I GREAT, OR WHAT!

## The GAP

Upon the conclusion of the sales transaction, most sales professionals neglect to request feedback on the quality of the service provided. As a result, they fail to learn from their mistakes and mature in their profession.

## The BRIDGE

In this Acceleration Strategy you'll discover why it's so important to obtain feedback from the client's service experience and how to go about getting it. In his acclaimed book *"The Ultimate Question"*, author Fred Reichheld discusses the merits of asking one single follow-up question at the conclusion of each sales transaction: "How likely are you to recommend my services to your friends and colleagues?" The rating scale ranges from 0 (not at all likely) to 10 (very likely).

The rating given in response to this ultimate question will reveal whether your past client is a *Net Promoter, Passive* (neutral), or *Net Detractor* of your product/ service offering.

According to Reichheld, *Net Promoters* are those who respond with a 9 or a 10. They are responsible for 80% of all repeat and referral business. They are the quiet foot soldiers campaigning on your behalf by actively endorsing you and your offering.

*Passives* represent those who respond to the "ultimate question" with a rating of 7 or 8. They don't actively endorse, nor do they actively denounce, your service offering. They are on the fence and

Bridging the SELLING Gap

won't hesitate to jump to whichever product/ service provider offers them a better price or more convenience. They have no product/ service loyalty.

*Net Detractors* are those who respond in the 0 to 6 range. Reichheld's research confirms that it is these people who are costing you the most. In fact, this group is responsible for 80% of the negative things said about you, your service, and the company you represent. Not only do they cost you in lost reputation but they cost you in lost time as well addressing their often loud and drawn out complaints.

Although the conclusion of any sales transaction represents a great opportunity for sales professionals to seek feedback, most don't. The reason is because they're afraid of what the response might bear out. After all, it can be somewhat humbling to have a client negatively critique the quality of your professional services, especially if your ego is closely associated to your professional competence.

During my twenty-year training career, I've made it a habit to obtain feedback after each and every training program I deliver, and in the process I've been humbled on a number of occasions. Initially stung by any unflattering comments received, I soon realized that each of these comments was a gift in disguise. In the long run, this feedback has allowed me to continually hone my craft and improve every aspect of my course content and delivery. Today my live training workshops typically generate a near-perfect 100% Net Promoter Score.

True greatness is achieved by doing, reviewing and taking corrective action on what's not working. The Apollo 11 crew discovered this fact on their journey to the moon. After the July 20, 1969, lunar landing, a reporter praised crew members Neil Armstrong and Buzz Aldrin for their piloting skills in landing their lunar module in the exact intended location of the moon, 384,000 kilometers away from their launch site at the Kennedy Space Center. Armstrong responded that they were actually off course "95 percent of the time" and that the only way they got to their final destination was by constantly correcting for the fact that they were always off course.

Likewise your success is accelerated when you learn from your mistakes and take course-correcting action. A customer satisfaction survey provides this opportunity; so don't let your ego get in the way of asking for feedback. The only bad feedback is the feedback you fail to obtain.

---

### SERVICE EXCELLENCE Tip:

**The only feedback is the bad feedback
you fail to obtain.**

---

Just as the Apollo 11 crew was able to pilot their spacecraft to their desired reality destination, so too will you get to where you want to get to in your business by engaging in course corrective behavior.

One of my Australian-based real estate clients has instituted a policy in which the Managing Director of each regional office is required to personally conduct a follow-up satisfaction survey on their clients. This initiative has been "extremely enlightening" and has provided them with three significant opportunities to accelerate the growth of their business:

1. The opportunity to gauge the performance of their individual sales agents and teams,
2. The opportunity to obtain valuable third party feedback to help improve performance, and
3. The opportunity to convert Net Detractors (dissatisfied customers) into Net Promoters (satisfied customers) by taking the necessary actions to make good on failed service experiences.

So consider conducting your own satisfaction survey, or commission someone else to conduct it on your behalf. While you should not expect to generate a 100% response rate from those surveyed, those who do are sure to provide you with insights that you need to help you hone your craft and direct your customer service training initiatives.

I appreciated IBM's Thomas J. Watson's response when asked how to achieve success more rapidly, "Double your failure rate" came his quick reply. Remember there are no such thing as failures; there are only distinctions.

## SERVICE EXCELLENCE ACTION PLAN

**o—►INSIGHTS:**

Know that your client is either a; *Net Supporter, Passive,* or a *Net Detractor* of your product/ service offering and that the only bad feedback is the feedback that you fail to obtain.

**o—►SKILLS:**

Apply a client satisfaction survey to obtain feedback into the customer experience and take action on the information you receive from the client.

**o—►RESOURCES:**

Create your own resource! After each and every sales trans-action ask your client for feedback then take action on what they tell you. Use these distinctions to course correct yourself into the top 1% of your industry.

## Excellence in Action – SERVICE EXCELLENCE

**The GAP**

Most companies talk a good talk of service excellence but very few deliver it.

**The BRIDGE**

One of my favorite companies to work with is Colliers International. When it comes to putting the client's needs first this commercial real estate company really gets it.

Their client-centric approach to running their business starts with CEO, Doug Frye and Chief Knowledge Officer Craig Robbins. Both Doug and Craig recognize their roles as being in service to *their* customers, which consist of 16,000 plus employees in 61 countries around the world. They don't just talk about service excellence ... they obsess over it. It's at the core of who they are and as a result it has become part of the corporate culture filtering across all sectors of the business.

This commitment to service excellence inspired the formation of Colliers University. Headquartered in Seattle, Washington CU pumps millions of dollars annually into training programs that teach employees how to exceed customer expectations by:

- Delivering a superior commercial outcome (building better bridges)
- Delivering a superior service experience (raising the service bar)

Sort through the curriculum of the Colliers University course catalogue and you'll discover that the majority of the courses are dedicated to showing their people how to become better at helping theirclientsgetwhattheywantinlife. Whilemostoftheircompetitors are reigning in their training budgets, Colliers continues to ramp up their educational investment by expanding their curriculum and distribution capabilities.

Colliers has figured out that the better they become at helping their clients achieve their real estate goals the more benefit they derive as a company. The key is that they focus on the client first, and the paycheck second. It's no wonder why they are one of the fastest growing and most profitable commercial real estate companies in the world.

## The Result

Ten years ago Colliers International was a virtual unknown in the global commercial real estate market. Over the past few years the company has accelerated into the number two spot, as reported in a 2012 survey of top global brands (source: The Lipsey Co.), and continues to gain ground on number one.

# SUMMARY

> *"Knowing is not enough, we must do.*
> *Willing is not enough we must apply."*
> – Johann Goethe

At the conclusion of every one of my live presentations I recite the above quote. After all, new skills and insights can only effect personal change if they are applied. Knowing them is simply not good enough.

Those who have applied the principles of the Gap Analysis Sales Model © into their business have experienced dramatic results. Many of my course graduates credit this training with launching their career. Once they began to apply the skills and insights within this book their business immediately accelerated and they never looked back.

Personally, I love to hear these success stories and the immense joy that always accompany them. Some of these testimonials have been included in the following pages.

Now that you have read this book, I consider myself a partner in your success. As such, I look forward to hearing about your own personal success stories as you incorporate these skill sets into your business.

Remember, we get what we want in life when we help others get what they want. My promise to you is that the content of this book will help you get both.

To your accelerated success!

Gerald G. Clerx

# Special Bonus Offer

Dear Reader,

As the purchaser of this book you are entitled to attend a future three part "Bridging the SELLING Gap" webinar to help visually reinforce the key concepts discussed within this book.

To claim this special offer, go to our website at <u>www.thegapanalysis.com/special book offer</u> and register for an upcoming webinar that fits conveniently into your time schedule.

# Speaking Engagements

Gerald G. Clerx has been called the "presentation guru" who truly practices what he preaches. He is consistently the highest rated speaker at any conference in which he participates. His *engaging*, *entertaining*, and *inspiring* presentation style make him one of most sought after speakers in his profession. The skills and insights he imparts are relevant and immediately applicable.

To have Gerald G. Clerx speak at your next event, email keynote@thegapanalysis.com or call 888.388.6388.

### Praise from course participants

"When it comes to training in sales and negotiation, there is simply no one better than Gerald Clerx. Gerald has trained my brokers on several occasions both here in the USA and abroad and the results are profound and measurable. In addition to the skills transfer in his courses, they are high energy, interactive, and above all...fun. Gerald is wonderful to work with and makes himself available even when he is not "on the clock". It is with pleasure that I recommend Gerald to any organization looking to improve the skills of their people."

David Pinsel - Managing Director - Los Angeles, USA

"Gerald's training series was an eye-opener and truly an inspirational experience for me. I have had the privilege to not only take part in 'BRIDGING the GAP' but also be able to witness the impact of Gerald's work over all employees of my company, sales and non-sales, who continue to benefit from this concept daily. The concept and the way Gerald delivers it to graduates is one of the most influential tools I have ever experienced in my industry."

Iglika Yordanova - Manager Retail Services - Sofia, Bulgaria

"I recently undertook 'BRIDGING the GAP' training series with Gerald Clerx over three days. It was the best single training session that I have ever attended and changed the way that I perform in my work environment for the better. Consequently, I am achieving results at work that I didn't think were possible. I would highly recommend undertaking the 'BRIDGING the GAP' training series if ever given the opportunity."

Stephanie Tine - Account Manager - Melbourne, Australia

"I have completed several courses with Gerald over the past 6 or 7 years and I can honestly admit I use the skills and techniques that he promotes in my business on a daily basis, as do many of my colleagues who have attended similar courses with Gerald. In preparing each pitch to win an appointment I continually find myself referring back to Gerald's advice; looking to both read my target and align my offering with what they are trying to achieve. I have found these strategies to be highly effective, winning us countless jobs that seemed unobtainable prior to our winning pitch."

Anthony White - Director of Sales - Brisbane, Australia

"Gerald is a fantastic presenter whose teachings have helped me excel not only in the workplace but also in my personal life. I look forward to taking Gerald's course for years to come." September 9, 2011.

Ted Mildon - Sales Associate – Vancouver, Canada

"In 18 years in the industry I have participated in numerous training courses and workshops. The two courses of Gerald's that I have participated in have been in have been amongst the most memorable. Very relevant content and great delivery. I look forward to the next one."

Simon Kersten - Managing Director - Wollongong, Australia

"I had the privilege to hear Gerald speak on presentation skills and the use of personality profiling to maximize sales presentation results. I was overly impressed with his style of communication and his ability to engage me in to his topic. I wish we could have had more time with Gerald to learn even more. However, I was surprised by how much I took away from his presentation in only a short amount of time. Gerald has given me techniques to implement that have changed my business tenfold!"

Melissa Molyneaux - Senior Associate - Reno, USA

"Gerald's 'BRIDGING the GAP' training sessions are the best I have encountered to date, as far as content and delivery are concerned. It was in fact the only sessions I have attended that accurately address the common issues professionals face accompanied by appropriate strategies to address them moving forward. The interactive components of this course were second to none. I currently use several of the techniques taught by Gerald on an ongoing basis and would have no hesitation in recommending Gerald and his 'BRIDGING the GAP' training exercises."

Marcel Elias - Sales Associate - Sydney, Australia

"Gerald's perspective on understanding the personalities of prospects that you may be presenting to, and his strategy for delivering a message, or "value proposition", has greatly improved my success rate in competitive pitches. Gerald's 'BRIDGING the GAP' structure has also helped me to guide discussions in meetings, and provide verbal answers to "on the spot" questions in a way that resonates with my clients and prospects. I would recommend Gerald Clerx training over any other sales training that I have had in 12 years of working as a sales representative for multi-national corporations."

Alan Doak - Sales Representative - Ottawa, Canada

"I attended a number of 'BRIDGING the GAP' training session which Gerald facilitated. Anyone who wants to improve their skill set in obtaining a better understanding on who their clients are, what they want and how to move them from their current reality to their desired reality, should make these training sessions a priority!!!"

Paul Fernandes - Director of Sales - Sydney, Australia

"Gerald is an articulate, succinct, and inspired instructor who has broadened my knowledge and understanding of assessment, presentation, and negotiations. I have taken a number of courses from Gerald both on-line and in person. I consider all of them valuable learning experiences."

John Lind - Sales Representative - Toronto, Canada

"I have undertaken numerous courses conducted by Gerald Clerx. The course relating to DISC profiling was very interesting and Gerald was able to provide real life examples of how this has worked for him. This course was informative and I was able to take away tools that I could use not only at work but also in my personal life. Gerald's style of coaching/ training is second to none. He is interactive with the class, humorous and likeable. I have no hesitation in recommending Gerald as a trainer and I will continue to undertake his courses throughout my career."

Amanda Anderson - Account Manager - Melbourne, Australia

"Gerald's 'BRIDGING the GAP' seminar is an excellent tool for Sales Professionals. It opened my eyes to how I was running my business currently and what I needed to implement into my day-to-day business to get the results I am looking for. A very worthwhile experience!"

Adam Kosoy - Vice President, NIS - Toronto Canada

"This was my second course with Gerald and I have to say that he has a unique ability to transfer the knowledge and experience, enough to positively energize all of the people he comes in contact with. Although extremely technically minded Gerald has the ability to communicate with simple, friendly language with a great sense of humor."

Kreso Rendeli - Client Manager - Zagreb, Croatia

"I have had the privilege of being trained by Gerald on several different courses, these training sessions have all been entertaining, informative and most of all productive which has resulted in my career accelerating to new levels. In recent times I have found the formulas taught through the courses to be invaluable in setting me apart from my competitors and allowing me to continue to grow my business and brand in a tighter market. I have no hesitation in recommending any of Gerald's courses to anyone!"

Paul Tierney - Director of Sales - Adelaide, Australia

"Gerald is a difference maker! His 'BRIDGING the GAP' workshop was incredibly helpful and will be the driver behind our office winning more pitches."

Yumi Prater - Sales Associate - Indiana, USA

"If you get the chance to participate in any of Gerald's courses I would highly recommend the opportunity. I recently participated in Gerald's 'BRIDGING the GAP' seminar for a second time and highly recommended anyone whose business is client driven to participate in this course. The course provides an excellent structure and flow which allows us to help our clients bridge their gaps when it comes to their needs. Gerald's presentation skills keep the group fully active and engaged in the entire days program which is hard to do with a large group, over a extended period of time."

Matt Saunders - Senior Associate - Vancouver, Canada

"Gerald's 'BRIDGING the GAP' training was probably one of the most memorable that I have attended, not only because Gerald is very talented presenter who connects with the audience in an instant, moreover because the course has changed my ability to win deals and gain partners forever. I have attended Gerald's course 3 times and every time I learn something new and valuable for me as a person and professional."

Verka Petkova - Manager Client Services - Sofia, Bulgaria

"Gerald, I recently went back to a client of mine in Bucharest, Romania. When I walked into his office I noticed that a presentation that I had submitted to him over a year ago was prominently displayed on his office bureau. When I asked why he still had my presentation out on display he replied "I use it as a constant reminder to myself of what an outstanding presentation should look like."

Blake Horsley - Sales Associate - Bucharest, Romania

Made in the USA
San Bernardino, CA
07 July 2013